ANISTATIA MILLER
&
JARED BROWN

SPIRITUOUS
JOURNEY

ANISTATIA MILLER
&
JARED BROWN

SPIRITUOUS
JOURNEY

CLEARVIEW BOOKS

C O N T E N T S

FOREWORD

The Mint Julep, I've always held, is a drink that causes fisty-cuffs in bars, mainly because nobody can agree on whether the mint should be muddled into the drink, or if, instead, it should sit daintily on top of the julep cup, acting as a glorious aromatic garnish. Hint: It's an aromatic garnish, but I'll fight to the death for your right to disagree. If you don't mind being wrong, that is.

Similarly, the Old-Fashioned Whiskey Cocktail is often the cause of heated debate when the question of whether or not to add fruit to the drink arises. "Man and boy I've built Old-Fashioned Cocktails these sixty years…and I have never yet had the perverted nastiness of mind to put fruit in an Old-Fashioned. Get out, scram, go over to the Palmer House and drink," admonished a crusty old bartender at the Drake Hotel in Chicago to a customer who had requested an Old-Fashioned without fruit. Controversial drinks such as these make the world of spirits and cocktails so darned interesting, right?

Spirituous Journey is bound to be controversial in some circles, too, and that's what makes it so much fun. I can see spirits and cocktail geeks in bars all over the world citing this book to back up their spirituous arguments. But the research that's been undertaken in order to bring us some of the most remarkable facts surrounding the very first distilled spirits, right through to the birth of the Cocktail in the early 1800s, has obviously been a work of love on behalf of Miller and Brown. They are a pair of cocktailian mavens if there ever was one.

I've been on a spirituous journey most of my life, so I wasn't too surprised when Jared and Anistatia asked me if I'd be interested in writing the foreword to this book. They know me well. "Send it on," I bade them, and one Saturday morning in May, 2009, I made myself a large cup of coffee, tucked into a chocolate doughnut, and devoured this fabulous tome in one sitting. My mind was boggled by the sheer volume information herein.

In order for me to write this foreword, Anistatia and Jared were forced to send me a text file containing all of the fascinating facts that you are about to discover. I envy you the hours that lie ahead. I, however, am now the proud owner of a searchable file that's packed with information that I'll no doubt steal for many projects of my own for years and years to come. Thanks Anistatia. Thanks Jared.

I hear that a second volume of this work will be published in the near future, and I'm hoping that I'm invited back to at least review the work. Miller and Brown's toils save me hours and hours of exhaustive research. And they make it so much fun to read, too.

With Much Love, from Gary Regan

PREFACE

We have been on a spirituous journey ever since we first met. To boldly quote author Edward Gorey, our obsession "came seventeen years ago – and to this day it has shown no intention of going away."

This won't start out like Charles Dickens' *David Copperfield*: "To begin my life with the beginning of my life, I record that I was born…". Oops. Sorry.

Our story starts when we first met in New York City on 17 December 1991, got engaged on 19 December 1991 and got married 31 January 1992. (There was a schedule conflict that kept us from reaching the altar any sooner.) We were married again for friends and family on Boxing Day 1992.

So what happens when two anoraks get together who both live with the moniker "walking encyclopaedia"? They go spotting together. Except there's a hitch. We aren't into watching trains, birds or planes. We have a more than healthy fascination with historical events and how they intersect with the invention and evolution of potent potables and the drinks made with them.

It didn't help that we were asked to revised a miscellany of historical events in chronological order for a speaker's reference book. It's amazing how you begin to see connections amongst seemingly unrelated events set against a day-by-day framework. Similar or related types of activities can and do take place on the same day separated by years, decades, even centuries. And it certainly didn't help when we were asked to write a sequel.

One more project set us on our never-ending path while we were living in Vancouver, Canada. Back in 1995, our literary agent (yes, we once had one) rung us up and suggested we do a web site on something, anything. We were just settling down to a couple of Martinis when the idea struck. Why don't we post all the trivia we know about one of our favourite subjects: Martinis? Well. A few quick runs through coding sites and a few sleepless nights, we had a web site. On Halloween night 1995 we launched *Shaken Not Stirred: A Celebration of the Martini*. We thought "maybe we'll get a few visitors." We had no idea that outside of Vancouver the world of potent potables was erupting. We still hadn't thought about it when an editor at HarperCollins asked us to write a book based on our site. We still didn't know – even when we went to New York to promote the book – that the drinks world had breached like a humpback whale from calm tropical seas.

All we knew was that we loved to comb the stacks at the Vancouver library, find old cocktail books in yard sales and used book shops, obsessively watch movies and a 1980s British TV series titled *The Day the Universe Changed: A Personal View*. Why that one in particular? Science historian James Burke presented how science and philosophy, the world and everything interconnect with each other. It became our guiding light as we dug up who invented what drink, who drank it, what was going on around the world while the drink was popular, why the spirit was invented anyway. We collected as many bits and pieces of information as we could, even if it meant keeping more than a couple of shoe-boxes and binders. By a sheer stroke of luck, data storage has evolved from index cards and notebooks to floppy disks to CDs to external hard drives and online data storage. Helps when you

couple all this data gathering with an equal number of years of hitting the road to discover even more bits and pieces in between presenting our findings to bartenders and just about anyone who would listen on three continents. Fortunately, most of them have had a drink in their hands when this happened.

The inspiration to put everything down on paper came in 2006 when we were asked to deliver two 3-day-long master classes on the history of drinks before an esteemed group of American and European bartenders on Île de Bendor in southern France. We realised it was time to put everything together once and for all. (Let's not talk about the fact that the class text was speed-written in 60 days.) That led to even more research and questioning of facts, both before and after that event.

By no means have we stopped picking and prodding through every single book, journal, magazine, movie and clipping we can get our hands on. We probably never will. Every year, every month, every day, every hour, we discover some new piece to add to the jig-saw puzzle. We learn a new truth, take a deep breath and correct our previous conclusions. (Remember: A good historian constantly looks for more of the truth and documents it at a certain point in time so that future historians can follow the trail in hopes of discovering more.)

We have more than a few people to thank for giving us the opportunity to dive into the deep end of this ocean of drinks history and having the patience to deal with us while we were writing it all down. First off, thanks to César Giron and the Worldwide Cocktail Club's Henry Besant and Dré Masso for convincing us to write and deliver that master class in southern France and then spend the past couple of years swimming through spirits history and the vast collection of bottles housed in Exposition Universelle des Vins et Spiritueux on Île de Bendor. A huge thanks to Nick Blacknell and Sue Leckie of Beefeater, Yves Schladenhafen of Havana Club and Jamie Terrell of Sagatiba for letting us write for them the histories of cachaça, British gin cocktails and Cuban rum, respectively, while we were developing this book.

Then, a hardy thanks to the other anoraks with whom we have exchanged tidbits of information with over the years including Dave Broom, Desmond Payne, Geraldine Coates, Nick Strangeway, Miranda Dickson, Jeff Masson, Charles Vexenat, Peter Dorelli, Salvatore Calabrese, Albert Montserrat, Eric Fossard, Ago Perrone and Dave Wondrich.

Finally, a huge hug to our copy editor Mardee Haidin Regan for making it look like we passed our grammar exams. And a huge Manhattan to some guy named Gary Regan for writing the foreword.

There you have it. That's how we got started, that's who helped us get there and here's where we are now.

This first book of *Spirituous Journey* is what we've recorded thus far about the invention of the different spirits categories and the birth of the Cocktail as we know it.

The second book will cover the evolution of the mixed drink from the Industrial Revolution to present day. Still sifting through more facts and controversies.

So make yourself a drink, sit back and enjoy this first pitstop along the road to perdition. We'll see again soon.

Cheers,
Anistatia Miller and Jared Brown

CHAPTER ONE
The Genie in the Bottle

SHARED KNOWLEDGE LEADS TO THE BIRTH OF ALCOHOL

A gift from the gods. A miracle cure. The secret to prolonging life. The Devil's brew. The destroyer of lives. Or as Americana historian Bernard DeVoto once put it, the backbone of the "pause in the day's occupation that is known as the cocktail hour." Alcohol has been all of these things and more during its long existence. Liquor, spirits, distillate, booze, whatever you call it, from the first moment that people gathered into social groups, created settlements and established institutions, alcohol has been part of the equation.

Who first coined the term "alcohol"? The fourteenth-century alchemist Ramon Llull believed this beverage "was destined to revive the energies of modern decrepitude." He divined the word from the old Arabic, *al kol* or *al ghol*, a loan word from the Vedic *khola* which was used to describe a whole genre of alcoholic beverages. According to a *Heart Views* article titled "Alcohol: Friend or Foe? A Historical Perspective",

Dr Rachel Hajar scoured ancient Arabic texts to discover the dual meanings of *al kol:* "1: a genie or spirit that takes on varied shapes (a supernatural creature in Arab mythology). 2: Any drug or substance that takes away the mind or covers it." Before alcohol captured the attention of European scholarship, the term had attained both mythical and medical status.

Many nineteenth-century etymologists led us to believe the provenance was the Arabic term *al kohl*, meaning powder of antimony, which women in the eastern hemisphere use to darken their eyelids: the world's first eye shadow. But it is difficult to see how a distillate of stibinite, a natural sulfide of the metalloid antimony, had anything to do with a potent potable that featured prominently in Asian medical practice and religious ritual.

Think about it: Nine thousand years ago, the Chinese made potions and perfumes by distilling essences, capturing the vapours of boiled flora or fauna in a catch-bowl, which was connected by a side-tube to a receiver. Anything that could harness volatiles that could be stored for future use was a major plus in a world lacking refrigeration and chemical preservatives. Naturally, neighbouring nations and trading partners quickly adapted the technique to suit the given environment and need.

This process was a natural progression from the practice of fermenting botanicals. Archeochemist Dr Patrick McGovern from the Museum of Applied Science Center for Archaeology at the University of Pennsylvania Museum of Archaeology and Anthropology in Philadelphia and a team of Chinese archaeologists uncovered the remains of one of these concoctions in the Neolithic Chinese village of Jiaju, one of the earliest sites associated with the egalitarian Peiligang culture. Dated to circa 7000BC, the excavated vessels contained remnants of a beverage fermented from rice, honey and fruit. That was around the same time Near Eastern cultures were brewing up and storing barley beer and wild grape wine. But then McGovern has excavated all sorts of interesting finds like this for about a decade now.

He exhumed tightly lidded bronze vessels in Anyang, China, filled with aromatised rice and millet wines macerated with wormwood, chrysanthemum, China fir, elemi and other herbs and flowers. They are dated from the Shang and Western Zhou dynasties (circa 1250–1000BC) and resemble ones described in some Shang dynasty oracle-bone inscriptions. Descendants of these early concoctions are still produced today in Vietnam as *ruou*, in China as *zieu* or *chiew*, in Korea as *shochu* and in Japan as *soju*. European descendants follow similar patterns: the *vinum hippocraticum* which was developed in ancient Greece and its eighteenth-century Italian offspring, vermouth.

One of the first cultures to adopt this new preservation technique were the nomadic Mongols, who employed a rudimentary method to produce *arkhi* from mare's milk, a drink that did not spoil in the harsh desert environment. Heated milk was allowed to ferment via wild yeast and then was repeatedly frozen to separate the "water" from the mixture. The collected liquid was approximately thirty percent ABV [alcohol by volume], meaning it could be safely stored and consumed for months.

Seventeenth-century American settlers used this same method in the frigid New England colonies to make applejack. (However, we do not recommend trying this yourself. The process also concentrates lethal congeners.)

More sophisticated societies encountered distillation around 3500BC as the Chinese vapour-collection technique travelled along the Silk Roads, by land and by sea, to India, to Southeast Asia, to Persia and to Egypt. Not just silk, spices, precious metals and gems were traded. Political emissaries, military personnel and scholars who traversed these routes carried an even more precious commodity: knowledge. Noodle-making, astrology, printing and especially alchemy (a study that combined diverse disciplines from chemistry, metallurgy, physics, medicine, astrology, astronomy and semiology, to art, music, philosophy, mysticism and spiritualism into one big package) made their way westward.

The alchemists. They were the guardians of an intellectual treasure chest that sought to explain the meaning of life, the earth, the secrets of the universe. Alchemy was science in its infancy. (It took centuries of passionate

political and religious prejudice for the term to become associated with witchcraft and devil-worship.) In the hands of the alchemists, distillation and alcohol gained new meaning on the Indian subcontinent.

THE LAND OF SOMA

Back to the Silk Road. The Chinese and Proto-Indo-Iranians (formerly called Aryans of India) had exchanged ideas and goods for about a thousand years by the time the world's oldest surviving documents, the Vedas, were written in Sanskrit around 2500BC. An attempt to document the knowledge that had been handed down through oral tradition, there are passages in the Vedas that detail how to make potable alcohol. One passage mentions the use of a ritual intoxicant called *somarasa* [liquor]. Oral tradition stated that it was made by the gods who distilled the juice of the somalatha plant (also used in Ayurvedic medicine for treating humans bitten by rabid animals). *Somarasa* was said to be the drink that made the gods immortal, especially Indra, the god of weather and war as well as chief deity. The Proto-Indo-Iranians consequently consumed *somarasa* in honour of Indra during religious festivals, especially the *somayajnas: atyanistama, uktya, sodasi, vajapeya, atiratra* and *aptoryama.*

As this sophisticated civilization morphed into the Hindu culture, distilled beverages became both spiritual and secular. In Kautilya's *Arthasastra*, a treatise on governing and economic policy written circa 500BC, a number of liquors are mentioned, including *medaka, prasanna, arita, maireya* and *madhu.* A particularly interesting spirit was *asava,* which was made from cereals, fruits, roots, barks, flowers or sugar cane, a plant native to Polynesia but farmed in China and India since antiquity. Four hundred years later, the *Susruta-Samhita,* the second of two volumes on Ayurvedic medicine, employed the word *khola* to describe all of these spirits.

To achieve a higher spiritual plane the ingestion of this psychoactive liquid meant that the imbiber could not only revere the gods but commune with them. They could achieve longevity and good health with this miraculous gift.

As the taste for alcohol increased, so did interest in improving the way it was made. Archaeological evidence was uncovered in northern India's Gandharan cities of Taxila and Charsadda that

by 150BC, distinct improvements were made to the design of stills used to produce liquor, while few were made to equipment used to extract mercury or other essences.

By this time, distillation had already reached Anatolia, Syria, Phoenicia, Gaza, Egypt, Bactria and Mesopotamia: all part of the Grecian Empire. Alexander the Great (356–323BC) and his generals embraced the effects of alcohol when they encountered it in northern India and exported the technique throughout the empire. Yet back in Greece, distillation was in its infancy, perceived as a means to collecting essence. However, a glimmer did appear on the intellectual horizon when Aristotle mused in his 350BC work *Meteorology* that:

Salt water when it turns into vapour becomes sweet, and the vapour does not form salt water when it condenses again. This I know by experiment. The same thing is true in every case of the kind: wine and all fluids that evaporate and condense back into a liquid state become water. They all are water modified by a certain admixture, the nature of which determines their flavour. But this subject must be considered on another more suitable occasion.

The art of the Chinese and Indian distillers took a slight detour to the south on its westward journey.

THE GREAT ALEXANDRIA LIBRARY

After the death of Alexander the Great, the Greco-Egyptian Empire became the fount of the world's knowledge of everything, including what was known of distillation. Ptolemy I Soter (367–282 BC), one of Alexander's generals who had accompanied him to Persia and India, imported the equipment and techniques to his new post in Egypt when he became ruler of Egypt's Hellenic dynasty in 323 BC. During his reign, one of his subjects Demetrius of Phalerum made an intriguing suggestion: establish a library of all the world's books. Ptolemy wanted to understand all the people of the Greco-Egyptian Empire, so housing Greek translations of Latin, Aramaic, Persian, Sanskrit, Hindu and Chinese became his obsession. He composed a letter to the empire's rulers begging them "not to hesitate to send him" works by authors of any and every kind. With this, the greatest repository of written knowledge in the ancient world, the Alexandria Library, was founded. An annex to the Hall of the Muses, the library, with Demetrius of Phalerum as its first librarian, was given the staggeringly difficult mission to acquire 500,000 written works.

Ptolemy's successors continued his legacy, but not always as forthrightly. There are tales of books being confiscated from visitors to Alexandria; of emissaries being sent throughout the Mediterranean to purchase old manuscripts. It is said that Ptolemy III borrowed the works of Aeschylus, Sophocles and Euripedes from the repository in Athens, leaving silver as collateral. He returned copies instead of the originals, telling the authorities they could keep the silver.

Before Egypt entered its Roman period, the Ptolemic dynasty had more than achieved its goal. The Alexandria Library boasted nearly 750,000 scrolls. The last of the dynasty's rulers, however, instigated the demise of the collection. After her ascent to the throne in 48BC, Cleopatra VII allowed Julius Caesar to help himself to the library's contents, which he did in hope of establishing his own great reference source. Tens of thousands of manuscripts were promptly shipped to Rome. Some stories say that Marc Antony donated 200,000 works from the library at Pergamum to replace what Cleopatra had frivolously given away.

The information flow ceased in 296AD, when Roman emperor Diocletian ordered the burning of the Alexandria Library's alchemical manuscripts to safeguard his economy. After all, the alchemists were trying to turn lead into gold and his treasury was based on a finite supply of the precious metal. If they succeeded, it would have meant the end of his empire.

An academic ember still flickered in the encroaching intellectual darkness. Hypatia and Zosimos, both of Alexandria, theoretically proposed that the four basic elements – fire, earth, air and water – could be transmutated through distillation around 300AD.

When Christianity enveloped the Roman Empire, it was not only a lack of funds and lack of public interest that took their toll on the great libraries. Throughout Europe, literacy became solely the domain of the teachers, scholars, alchemists and especially monks. As the public libraries closed, books were moved to the growing number of monasteries emerging as the empire declined. Christian fervour prompted one group of monks to sack the Alexandria

Library's remaining contents in 389BC. Greek, Arabic and Aramaic were deemed pagan languages, providing comprehensible information to the general public and too much temptation for academic minds who were expected to dedicate their energies to less secular topics. Thus the remnants of a few centuries of pooled knowledge went up in smoke.

Fortunately, a handful of monarchs and less-zealous monks did not completely embrace this constricted view. Within the cloistered walls of monasteries from Constantinople to Lisbon copies of the Alexandria Library's remarkable wealth were protected and were freely exchanged. Anyone who could still read those languages – after Latin was deemed Europe's scholarly tongue – could continue the quest for enlightenment in secret.

That is how budding European pharmacologists during the sixth and seventh centuries dredged up copies of Greek physician Pedanius Dioscorides' *De Materia Medica*, which was the basis for pharmacology for nearly 1,500 years after its publication in the first century AD. That is how European alchemists of the same era learned to distil turpentine and administer it as a medicine. That is how they learnt how to make *vinum hippocraticum*, Hipporcates's simple cure for intestinal worm infestation as well as digestive and flatuelence remedy. Dioscorides documented how he covered a clay vase with several layers of wool and suspended it on a wooden rack over a fire. To collect the distillate, he simply squeezed the liquid out of the wool. The distiller's art took three steps backward and a left turn to Mongolia by the late seventh century. Fortunately, an epiphany occurred in a rising new empire.

CHAPTER TWO
The Philosopher's Stone

SEEKING IMMORTALITY & DISCOVERING THE ALEMBIC

Knowledge thrived and flourished in the Near and Middle East as the Dark Ages descended upon Europe. The eighth century was the dawn of the Islamic Renaissance: a time when the Arab world made some of history's greatest intellectual and scientific leaps. Before the end of the 1200s, Muslim thinkers contributed numerous enhancements to the sciences, the arts and technology of every known culture with which they made contact.

Thousands of years of distillation had not yet yielded a pure or nearly pure result in the hands of the Chinese or Indians. In the hands of an Arab alchemist, alcohol experienced a metamorphic transformation. During the early dawn of the Islamic Empire, Abu Musa Jabir ibn Hayyan (aka: Geber, al-Jabir; circa 721–815) designed and successfully employed a new type of distillation device of his own design which was fitted with two retorts. He called his invention a *taqtir* or *al-ambiq*.

We now call this device an alembic still: a radical departure from early instruments because it concentrated more vapour and cooled the liquid to collect more alcohol.

Unlike the freeze distillation method or the employment of a catch-bowl to collect rising vapours, the alembic connected two retorts via a tube or neck. (Actually, the upper portion of each retort was called an alembic, while the lower portion of the retort was called a cucurbit. But throughout history the entire apparatus was given the name of the upper portion.) What made this device special was that the neck acted as a condenser that allowed the vapours to concentrate and flow along the neck to the receiving retort.

Inspired by the translated works of Zosimos of Panopolis, this scholar searched for a legendary substance that could transmute base metal into gold and prolong life: the philosopher's stone.

At first, he experimented with wine and salt, distilling them in his *al-ambiq*. In his treatise *Kitab ikhraj ma fi al-quwwa ila al-fi'l* [The Book of Obtaining from What Was in the Power to the Action] he documented:

And fire which burns on the mouths of bottles due to boiled wine and salt, and similar things with nice characteristics which are thought to be of little use, these are of great significance in these sciences.

Besides being one of the best all-around alchemists of his day, al-Jabir was methodical to the core. He evangelized on the importance of systemised experimentation. He distilled and consequently discovered hydrochloric acid, sulphuric acid, nitric acid, acetic acid, tartaric acid and citric acid while seeking the critical ingredients needed to make the Philosopher's Stone.

Al-Jabir did find a substance that could uncover gold hidden in lesser elements: *aqua regia* – the combined distillates of hydrochloric and sulphuric acids. (Though he first created it by combining common salt with vitriol, *aqua regia* not only melts gold, it is used even to this day to extract gold from other base ores.) Not quite the Philosopher's Stone, but

a valuable find nonetheless. Though he did not realise it or reap the anticipated monetary benefits, in a very real sense he also found a secret to prolonging life, which was another purpose of the Philosopher's Stone.

A few centuries after al-Jabir's death, it was widely believed that alcohol was safer to drink than water, thus prolonging life. Water was rightfully considered a dangerous substance through the Dark Ages well into the Victorian Era. It was suspected of causing a variety of troublesome, chronic and even terminal illnesses. Untreated water supplies in urban and rural areas contained a host a pathogens: E. Coli, giardia, cholera, typhoid, dysentery, cryptosporidium. As microscopic organisms had not been discovered, they did not know why alcohol worked, just that it worked.

Such was life before modern water treatment, since especially as villages, towns and cities grew, liquor became fundamental to survival by improving digestive health. Legend has it that the phrase "How do you do?" is a contraction of "How are your bowels today?" as it was also assumed at the time (and not entirely incorrectly) that the core of one's moods were located in the bowels.

Eventually some alchemists postulated that alcohol was "the good creature of God": vital to maintaining balance among the body's four humours or temperaments – sanguine, melancholic, choleric and phlegmatic – as described by the Greek physician Galen in 190AD.

THE BEST MAN OF HIS TIME

Yemenite alchemist Abu-Yusuf Ya'qoub ibn 'Ishaq ibn al-Sabbah ibn 'Omran ibn Isma'il al-Kindi (circa 801–873) recognized the significance of al-Jabir's work, but at a price.

Historian Ibn al-Nadim (d. 955) described al-Kindi as "the best man of his time, unique in his knowledge of all the ancient sciences." Educated in Kufa and then Baghdad, al-Kindi was fortunate to have both Abbasid caliphs al-Ma'mun and al-Mu'tasim as patrons. He was appointed to the House of Wisdom – the Alexandria Library of the Islamic world – where he translated Greek texts such as Zosimos's works on transmutation and distillation. Surrounded by a wealth of research sources, al-Kindi wrote over 260 treatises on topics that ultimately affected civilisation's understanding of the world.

It was al-Kindi who first introduced both the Islamic and Christian worlds to the Hindu numeral system: the base 10 standard that still is employed today. It was al-Kindi who developed cryptology, the science of decipherment. It was al-Kindi who introduced the concept of music therapy. And it was al-Kindi who defied a major tenet of alchemy, questioning the theory of transmutation.

He may not have believed base metal could be turned into gold, but based on al-Jabir's work, al-Kindi did believe a digestible *al'iksir* [elixir; water of life] could be derived from wine. The pivotal point in the development of beverage alcohol occurred when al-Kindi created brandy, the distillate of wine, using al-Jabir's *al-ambiq*. In his treatise, *Kitab al-Taraffuq fi al-'itr* [The Book of the Chemistry of Perfume and Distillations], al-Kindi detailed the process, concluding that "in the same way, one can distil wine in a water-bath and it comes out the same colour as rose water."

He took the process a critical step further (aside from not blending wine with salt). He isolated ethanol, collecting it at above 90 percent purity, according to some sources. (It took another millennium before absolute ethanol was collected.) In another study, al-Kindi offered up 107 potable spirits recipes plus a revised design for the alembic in his *Kitab Kimya Al-'Itr wa Al Tas'idat* [Book of Perfume Chemistry and Distillation].

For al-Kindi, fame for his intellectual discoveries was fleeting. When caliph al-Mutasim's son, al-Wathiq, came to power in 842, al-Kindi found he had more enemies than friends in high places. Pro-orthodox factions came into power, determined to cleanse the empire of radicals who questioned the interpretation of the Qu'ran. Intellectuals such as al-Kindi were accused of religious heresy during this Inquisition-like period in Islamic history.

Al-Kindi was publicly flogged for contesting fundamentalist beliefs about the Creation. His library was temporarily confiscated. When al-Wathiq's brother, al-Mutawakkil, came to power five years later, scholarship took a further back seat as the new caliph focused his energies on building the world's largest mosque, the Great Mosque of Samarra. Meanwhile, strong religious rivalries in the House of Wisdom took their toll on al-Kindi's credibility. By the time caliph al-Mu'tamid came to power in 870, al-Kindi was described as a "lonely man." Three years later, he died in relative obscurity.

The writings of Abu Nasr Muhammad ibn al-Farakh al-Farabi (aka: al-Farabi; 872–951) and Abu Ali al-Husayn ibn Abd Allah ibn Sina (aka: Avicenna; 980–1037) eventually overshadowed al-Kindi's formidable body of work on the subjects of music, metaphysics, medicine and distillation. Applying al-Kindi's theories, Ibn-Sina (aka: Avicenna) developed a steam distillation process, which he used to create essential oils. For this achievemenet, he is often regarded as the father of aromatherapy.

At the peak of the High Middle Ages (1000–1300), European scholars began translating the works of these Islamic thinkers into Latin and Greek. Sadly, al-Kindi's treatises were not widely circulated. Most copies of his work were destroyed during the 1200s when countless Islamic libraries were burned during the Mongol invasion of Persia and Arabia.

MEDICAL BENEFITS

One thing is certain: Al-Kindi's experiments planted a kernel of inspiration in the mind of Persian alchemist Abu Bakr Muhammad ibn Zakariya Razi (aka: al-Razi or Rhazes; 865–925). Born in Rayy, near Teheran, al-Razi studied music before turning his interest toward medicine. He headed the first Royal Hospital before moving to Baghdad to direct the Muqtadari Hospital. It was in this setting, al-Razi made some of his greatest clinical observations. He defined the differences amongst smallpox, chickenpox and measles. He employed diet as a form of medical treatment. In his work, *Kitab-al-Asrar* [The Book of Secrets], he introduced the use of mortars, flasks, spatulas and phials in the preparation of compounds. Al-Razi confirmed that volatile oils from herbs, spices, alkaloids and resins could be more easily administered in an alcohol base. In clinical trials, he determined alcohol improved the absorption of the medicinal properties and that it was an excellent preservative, inhibiting fermentation and the decomposition of prepared medication. Before he made these breakthrough discoveries, most maladies were treated with folk remedies or with magic.

Sadly, his major work, *Kitab al-Hawi fi al-tibb* [The Comprehensive Book on Medicine], in which he described many of his methods and observations, brought his brilliant career to an end. In his manuscript, al-Razi also contradicted the tenets of an important mullah, who ordered him to be beaten over the head with the treatise until one of them broke. As a result of the punishment, al-Razi suffered permanent blindness.

ENTER THE MOORS

A wave of knowledge crashed through an edge of the cloistered environment of Europe in 711 when the Umayyad Moors invaded and conquered the Iberian Peninsula. Spain and Portugal became known as al-Andalus for the next four centuries, a European showcase of all the jewels of the Islamic Renaissance. The city of Córdoba was fitted out with public baths, air-conditioned and heated buildings, street lights and perfumes. The citizens drank distillates made from wine and had loads of lovely books that explained how to make them.

The neighbouring Franks led by Charlemagne eschewed this pagan knowledge, holding fast to their Christian beliefs that anything handed down from the Greeks, Romans, Egyptians, let alone Muslims was taboo.

A buffer zone was created between France and Spain. Known as the Marca Hispanica, the region included Hispania, Toulouse and Gothia, stretching from Barcelona in Spain to Toulouse and

Nîmes in France. It was within this zone, that a wholly unique intellectual interchange occurred thanks to the intercessions of a single pope.

Unlike Emperor Diocletian and most Christian leaders before him, Pope Sylvester II (aka: Gerbert d'Aurillac; 950–1003) was not opposed to non-Christian knowledge. He had been educated in Moorish Spain and some historians believe he even studied alchemy in Córdoba and Sevilla. What is documented is that he was a French-Sephardic Jew by birth and upbringing. (This later contributed to accusations that Sylvester II was in league with Satan.) But because of Sylvester II's open-mindedness western civilization savoured its first taste of Islamic astronomy and mathematics. The pope requested that Arabic numerals replace the clumsy Roman ones. He also encouraged Christian scholars to discover the secrets of the Islamic alchemical texts. In this unique atmosphere, the academic world residing in the Marca Hispanica maintained a running dialogue that was free of religious prejudice or sanction.

Robert of Chester, who lived in Segovia, was one of these fortunate scholars.

In 1144, he finished translating and compiling many of al-Jabir's, al-Kindi's and al-Razi's distillation treatises into the book *Liber de Compositione Alchimae*. When this volume made its way into the hands of European alchemists such as Magister Salernus at the Academy of Salerno, the secret formulae for what was called *aqua ardens* [strong water] were written in code in the 1160 volume *Compendium Salerni*.

Universities were in their infancy. The University of Bologna, considered the oldest university in the western world, opened in 1088 and specialised in law. But the seats of innovation and experimentation rested elsewhere: in Paris' La Sorbonne (1200), in the universities of Oxford and Montpellier (1220), at Padua and Pales (1224), at Cambridge (1225) and Toulouse (1229) and at Salamanca (1230). It is within these hallowed halls that distillation made its next transformation.

CHAPTER THREE
The Water of Life

WESTERN CIVILIZATION DISCOVERS DISTILLATION

How did the phrase *aqua vitae* [*eau-de-vie*, in French] and the term "alcohol" come into common parlance? Arnaud de Ville-Neuve (circa 1235–1313) and three of his contemporaries take credit for transforming the mysterious al *kol* – "the substance that takes away the mind" – and the medical *khola* into the romantic and somewhat spiritual *aqua vitae* [water of life].

Between 1250 and 1269, these men not only successfully developed a new way to distil alcohol, but gave it life and new meaning.

BUT SOME NAME IT

Both spain and france claim de Ville-Neuve as a native son. The Spanish say he was born in the Catalan village of Villaneuva, while the French declare his birthplace was Villeneuve-Loubet near Nice. He is known in both countries by a myriad of other names and spellings: Arnaldus de Villa Nova, Arnaldus de Villanueva, Arnaldus Villanovanus, Arnaud de Villeneuve and Arnau de Vilanova.

What is known of his early life is that he began his education in Barcelona under the tutelage of John Casamila, a celebrated professor of medicine. There, de Ville-Neuve was attracted to the discoveries of Claudius Galen (129–216) and al-Razi (865–925).

In his 1310 book, *Liber de Vinis* [Book of Wine], de Ville-Neuve documented his method for distilling wine with an alembic. He termed the result *aqua vine* [water of wine] but noted that:

> *...some name it aqua vitae and this name is remarkably suitable since it is really a water of immortality. Its virtues are beginning to be recognised, it prolongs life, clears away ill-humours, revives the heart, and maintains youth.*

His excitement over such a miraculous discovery was obvious. Yet it proved not to be such an exaggeration a couple of centuries later. *Liber de Vinis* was a best seller and the term *aqua vitae* stuck. (In this same tome, he also advised readers that the optimal circumstance for tasting wine was: "… in the morning after they have rinsed their mouths and eaten three or four bites of bread dipped in water.")

De Ville-Neuve also perfected the mutage process. By adding spirits to wine to halt fermentation and preserve the liquid's natural sweetness, he originated *vin doux naturel*, predecessor to vermouth and other fortified wines. But by the time deVille-Neuve distributed these findings, the scales of religious sentiment tilted toward conservatism and fundamentalism.

Beginning in 1248, attempts were made by King Louis IX to forge a Franco-Mongol alliance with the Great Khan Güyük Khan and his successor Möngke in hopes of crushing the Islamic Empire's holdings in the Near East. None the negotiations came to fruition. Similarly, in 1267, Pope Clement IV (1195–1268) corresponded with Mongol Ilkhanate ruler Abaqa, hoping to form a crusade comprised of Christian French, Mongols and Byzantines led by Abaqa's father-in-law Emperor Michael VIII Palaeologos. The crusade never came to fruition.

Under Pope Clement V (1264–1314), the seat of the Roman Catholic Church moved from Italy to France. The powerful Knights Templar was abolished strictly for political reasons. Then the Medieval Inquisitions (Episcopal Inquisition [1184–1230s] and the Papal Inquisition of the 1230s) deemed all forms of non-Christian thought to be heresy. This placed de Ville-Neuve and his work under close scrutiny.

At the height of his career de Ville-Neuve was regarded as the best physician and alchemist of his day and attended to the health needs of popes Innocent V, Boniface VIII, Benedict IX and Clement V as well as monarchs Pedro III and James II of Aragon, Robert of Naples and Frederick II of Sicily. He even served as vice-chancellor of the University of Montpellier while teaching medicine, botany and general alchemy. But in his later years, de Ville-Neuve's life more closely resembled that of al-Kindi. His fame garnered numerous enemies among ecclesiastics and scholars. He was accused of heresy in 1309, based on his comments about the Mass, the Antichrist, Jesus Christ and Armageddon. Following is one such passage from his book *De Fine Mundi*:

The charitable works and services rendered to humanity by a good and wise physician are preferable to everything that priests call good works, prayers, or even the holy sacrifice of the mass.

De Ville-Neuve was exiled by inquisitions in both Spain and Paris. He found asylum in Sicily. Pope Clement V warned his friend and physician: "You will gain our respect if you concentrate on medicine and leave theology alone." Around 1313, Clement called de Ville-Neuve to return to the papal seat at Avignon. On his way to the pontiff's side, his vessel was shipwrecked. De Ville-Neuve died in the catastrophe and was buried in Genoa. (It is interesting to note that although de Ville-Neuve passed away without receiving the Church's respect, his daughter who had become a nun was canonized and became Saint Rosalie.)

Collected editions of de Ville-Neuve's works were not printed and published until 1504 in Lyon, France. But three of de Ville-Neuve's contemporaries and colleagues are known to have spread the word about aqua vitae.

DOCTOR ILLUMINATUS

Ramon Llull (1232–1315) is said to have learned the secrets of distillation and the production of the Philosopher's Stone directly from de Ville-Neuve. Born in Mallorca, Llull was a well-educated nobleman and a tutor to James II of Aragon before he had a religious epiphany and became a hermit from 1265 until 1274. As Arthur Schopenhauer recounted in his 1819 work, *The World as Will and Representation*:

Hence men who have led a very adventurous life under the pressure of passions, men such as kings, heroes, or adventurers, have often been seen suddenly to change, resort to resignation and penance, and become hermits and monks. To this class belong all genuine accounts of conversion, for instance, that of Ramon Llull, who had long wooed a beautiful woman, was at last admitted to her chamber, and was looking forward to the fulfillment of all his desires, when, opening her dress, she showed him her bosom terribly eaten away with cancer. From that moment, as if he had looked into hell, he was converted; leaving the court of the King of Mallorca, he went into the wilderness to do penance.

Returning from seclusion, Llull entered the Franciscan order where he was valued for his linguistic abilities in Latin,

Catalan, Occitan and Arabic. Like de Ville-Neuve, he taught at Montpellier and La Sorbonne. It was there that he had a few encounters with Oxford don John Duns Scotus, who went by the honorific name Doctor Subtilis.

Most historians agree the two scholars were at the same universities from 1291 to 1296 as well in 1302. It was Duns Scotus who dubbed Llull "Doctor Illuminatus." (According to George Sarton in volume three of his *Introduction to the History of Science*, Llull was encouraged to visit Britain's King Edward II, in 1297, to explain the secrets of the Philosopher's Stone and subsequently, distillation. But not all Llull scholars record that such a sojourn was ever made.)

As an alchemist, Llull's interests did not lean as deeply into mysticism as those of his colleagues. His studies led to the development of a debating tool intended to win the Muslims over to Christianity through logic and reason. This method was based on a device employed by Arab astrologers, the *zairja*, which determined the meaning of thoughts through the association of numbers to letters and topics. (Llull did not unveil this system until 1305 in his work *Ars generalis ultima* [aka: *Ars magna*]).

Like his predecessors, Llull suffered for his progressive thinking. He was vocally opposed for his radical views on rational mysticism by Grand Inquisitor Nicolau Aymerich. That naturally led to his exile from Spain. Yet, he continued his attempts to convert the Muslims to Christianity. So Llull sailed to Tunisia in 1307 to preach Christianity. As a result of his efforts, he was imprisoned there for six months and then expelled from the country.

Llull worked from his home in Mallorca over the course the next seven years, ultimately achieving one of his dreams. He convinced church leaders to establish linguistic education departments through Europe. The Council of Vienne ordered, in 1311, the creation of chairs at the Papal Court in Hebrew, Arabic and Chaldean. The decree also established similar chairs at the universities of Bologna, Oxford and Salamanca, as well as La Sorbonne.

He returned to North Africa in 1314, to preach Christianity in Béjaïa. But this time the 82-year-old professor met with fatal opposition: He was stoned by an angry Muslim crowd. Llull was transported back to his home in Mallorca by Genoese merchants trading in the area. He died from his injuries a year later.

Of the more than 260 works Llull wrote during his lifetime, there is one passage that most eloquently defined de Ville-Neuve's "water of life." In his book *Secunda Magia Naturalis*, Llull described *aqua vitae* as "an element newly revealed to man, but hid from antiquity because the human race was then too young to need this beverage which was destined to revive the energies of modern decrepitude."

But besides giving the liquid a memorable definition and a name that we still use today, Llull contributed the theory of double-distillation. In his posthhumously-published 1330 work, *Experimenta*, Llull documented how to take *aqua vitae* "of the highest strength such that it burns a linen cloth and to again put it through the alembic."

Despite his run-ins with the Roman Catholic Church, Llull was beatified in 1858, but never canonized. And although he was given an honorific name, he was never conferred as one of the 33 Doctors of the Church.

There was another doctor who might have provided both de Ville-Neuve and

Llull with the inspiration to pursue *aqua vitae*, Doctor Mirabilis.

DOCTOR MIRABILIS

Roger Bacon (1214–1294), also delved into the mysteries of aqua vitae while translating al-Razi's *Kitab Sirr al-Asrar* [Secret of Secrets], which he published, in 1280, under the Latin title *Secretum Secretorum*. A master at Oxford University who lectured on Aristotle, Bacon also taught at La Sorbonne from 1237 to 1245. Is it a coincidence that Bacon translated al-Razi and taught at La Sorbonne where a few decades later de Ville-Neuve and Llull taught and conducted research? We think not. La Sorbonne attracted numerous alchemical and philosophical scholars whose works were liberally shared within the university communities. Bacon's translation would not have gone unnoticed by the likes of any alchemist, let alone de Ville-Neuve and Llull.

When he entered the Franciscan order around 1256, Bacon was restricted from publishing any of his studies without specific approval. Adding injury to insult, he was no longer allowed to teach at a university. But thanks to his acquaintanceship with Pope Clement IV, he was permitted to write his *Opus*

Magnus [Great Work] as well as a few tomes on alchemy and astrology.

Like his contemporaries, Bacon also found himself in trouble with the Church. During the late 1270s, he was placed under house arrest by the head of the Franciscan order, Jerome of Ascoli, because of his research into deterministic astrology and other taboo topics. Upon his return to Oxford sometime after 1278, Bacon continued his studies without communication to the outside world until his death 16 years later.

Because of Bacon's translation of al-Razi's work, the seeds of distillation knowledge were planted in Britain, too. Most certainly they sprouted as John Duns Scotus returned to Oxford with news of de Ville-Neuve's and Llull's discoveries a few decades later.

We know that this improved form of distillation quickly travelled, by 1320, from Britain to Ireland. That is when Bishop Richard Ledred recorded in his diocese's register, known as the *Red Book of Ossory*, that:

> *Simple aqua vitae is to be made in the following manner: take choice one year old wine, and rather of a red than of a thick sort, strong and not sweet, and place it in a pot, closing the mouth well with a clepsydra made of wood, and having a linen cloth rolled round it; out of which pot there is to issue a cavalis leading to another vessel having a worm. This latter vessel is to be kept filled with cold water, frequently renewed when it grows warm and the water foams through the cavalis. The pot with the wine having been placed previously on the fire, distil it with a slow fire until you have from it one half of the quantity of wine that you put in.*

The Irish called the result by its Gaelic name *uisce-beatha*. We now know it as whiskey. Around this time, the verb *bous* or *bouse* [to drink to excess] first appeared in the English language, derived from the Middle Dutch verb *busen* [to drink liquor to excess], a close relation to the Middle High German term busen [to revel or carouse]. (The word "booze" became a noun during the 1850s when EG Booz of Philadelphia marketed his namesake whiskey in log-cabin bottles which were reproduced a century later by the Old Mr Boston.)

DOCTOR UNIVERSALIS

The third and last of de Ville-Neuve's contemporaries to embrace the art of distillation was the German Dominican friar Albertus Magnus (1206–1280). This particular teacher of alchemy, theology and philosophy bridged the cavernous gap between science and religion. Against his family's wishes, Magnus entered the Dominican order around 1223 and studied in Bologna before becoming a lecturer at the University of Cologne. In 1245, he accepted a position at La Sorbonne, where he no doubt encountered Roger Bacon. During his tenure there, his most famous student was St Thomas Aquinas, who was also known as "Doctor Angelicus."

Dubbed "Doctor Universalis," Magnus's study of distillation may well have been triggered by Bacon's translation of al-Razi and led to the publication of his own experiments in his *Compositum de composites*, in which he described the process:

Leave it to ferment, the impurities drop to the bottom and the water passes from yellow to red. At this time, you will retrieve the flask and you will put it over the cinders of a very mild fire. Adapt to it the head of the alembic with a recipient. Begin the distillation slowly. That which passes, bit by bit, is our Water of Life. A very clear, pure, heavy, virginal milk, a very sour Vinegar. Continue the fire gently until all the water of life has distilled gradually over. Then, stop the fire, let the furnace cool and conserve with care your distilled water. This is it: Our Water of Life, Vinegar of the Philosophers, Virgin's Milk which reduces the bodies to their first matter, It was given an infinity of names.

Ordained as a bishop by Pope Alexander IV in 1260, Magnus returned home to Germany as a highly respected member of the Church and a venerated scholar. Unlike his colleagues who died in disgrace or were little more than exonerated, Magnus was beatified and canonized – like his student Aquinas. It goes without saying that Magnus's published experiments introduced Germany and the rest of northern and eastern Europe to the art of distillation.

There were two other influences that catapulted interest in beverage alcohol beyond anyone's dreams. This time, they came via the Italian cities of Genoa and Venice.

CHAPTER FOUR
In the Land of Arrack

THE MERCHANTS OF ITALY & MARCO POLO

The exotic orient once again was a protagonist in the maturation and evolution of beverage alcohol as the Crusades brought Europeans close to the border of the Land of Green Ginger. The Crusades (1095–1291), a series of Vatican-sanctioned military conflicts aimed at wresting the Holy Land and the city of Jerusalem away from the Islamic Empire, stoked interest in the wealth of Asia: silks, spices and opiates. These treasures were so valued in the European courts that Venetian and Genoese merchants established major trade contracts as early as the eleventh century and maintained a steady flow of sumptuous items for their affluent clientele.

The writings of two early Christian missionaries titillated public interest in the Orient, as historian William Stevenson recorded in his 1824 book, *Robert Kerr's General History and Collection of Voyages and Travels, Volume 18*:

In the years 1245, 1246, the pope [Innocent IV] sent ambassadors to the Tartar and Mogul khans: of these [John de Plano] Carpini has given us the most detailed account of his embassy, and of the route which he followed. ...Besides the information derived from his own observations, he inserts in his narrative all he had collected; so that he may be regarded as the first traveller who brought to the knowledge of western Europe these parts of Asia; but though his travels are important to geography, they throw little light on the commerce of these countries.

[William de] Rubruquis was sent, about this time, by the king of France to the Mogul emperor:... He is the first traveller who mentions koumis [a fermented beverage from mare's milk sometimes distilled to make arkhi or arika] and arrack...

In 1248, William de Rubruquis of Flanders (aka: William de Rubrouck; William de Rubroeck; 1220–1293) accompanied King Louis IX on the Seventh Crusade. Per Louis' orders, he set out on 7 May 1253 from Constantinople to convert the Tartars to Christianity. De Rubruquis followed the route of Hungarian Friar Julian, accompanied by Bartolomeo da Cremona, an attendant called Gosset and an interpreter named Homo Dei or Abdullah [man of God]. The group crossed this unknown world, reaching Karakorum, the capital of the Mongol Empire, and returning with tales of wonder.

Reports like those by Carpini and de Rubruquis stoked the embers of curiosity in ambitious merchants such as Maffeo and Niccolò Polo. The brothers initially plied their wares in Venice. But in 1251, they moved to Constantinople to get closer to the Muslim traders who transported goods via the Silk Road land routes. Eight years later, they moved to the Crimea, which was another commercial hub. Finally, in 1266, they moved to the source of some of their most prized imports – Khanbaliz [Beijing], home of the great Mongol emperor Kublai Khan.

In his book, *Il Milione* (literally "The Millions", later titled *The Travels of Marco Polo*), Niccolo's son Marco Polo

(1254–1324) explained how Kublai Khan favourably received the family and sent them back with a letter addressed to Pope Clement IV, requesting that 100 educated people be sent to China to teach Christianity and western customs to his people. In the same document, the khan also asked for a container of oil from the lamp of the Holy Sepulchre in Jerusalem. The letter was accompanied by a *paiza*, a 12-by-3 inch golden tablet that authorized the bearer to request from anyone and obtain without question lodging, horses and food throughout the khan's dominion.

By the time the Polos returned to Venice, in 1268, political upheaval delayed their audience at the Vatican. Pope Clement IV had died and conflicts between the French and Italian cardinals delayed the election of a new pontiff. This was quickly followed by the Eighth Crusade, led by Louis IX of France. The campaign transformed the European political arena.

Asked by the Papal Legate Cardinal Ottobono to join Louis IX in this endeavour, Prince Edward of England went into debt to join his friend and advance their combined forces into Acre, Israel. Louis died in Tunis, triggering a dispute back home amongst his brother

Charles of Anjou, King Hugh III, the Knights Templar and the Venetians.

Louis' death left Edward no choice but to continue on to the Ninth Crusade in 1271. Among those who rode with Edward was his friend Theobald Visconti. Much to his surprise, that same year Visconti was elected pontiff and enthroned as Pope Gregory X. Edward returned to Britain the following year, to take the throne after the death of his father King Henry III.

Immediately after his enthronement, Pope Gregory X received the Polos. The family – accompanied by 17-year-old Marco and two Dominican monks, who were all the teachers the pontiff could afford to send – returned to China, delivering the oil from the Holy Sepulchre. In return, the Mongol Ilkhanate sent a delegation of 12 representatives to the 1274 Council of Lyon to discuss military cooperation between Christian Europe and the Mongol Empire. But two years later, plans for a Tenth Crusade died along with Pope Gregory X.

For 17 years, the Polo family lived in China. A gifted storyteller, young Marco was a court favourite. According to his memoirs, he was given many diplomatic jobs. He received his final mission, in 1291, when Kublai Khan ordered him to escort Princess Koekecin and her wedding party to her fiancée Ilkhan Arghun. The khan also granted the Polos leave to return home to Venice.

The family travelled by sea for two years, sailing from Quanzhou through Sumatra to Sri Lanka and India before reaching to the Ilkhanate, today's Iran, Iraq, Afghanistan, Turkmenistan, Armenia, Azerbaijan, Georgia, Turkey and western Pakistan. In the second volume of his memoirs, Marco described the wonders found in the Indonesian trading ports of Samara, Dagroian and Basman. (Dutch anthropological linguist HKJ Cowan determined, in 1948, that these three ports were actually Samalanga, Pidie and Peusangan that are located in the Aceh region of Sumatra.)

Of the many discoveries Polo recounted, one is of particular interest: a local beverage not dissimilar to the asava made in India and the arrack discovered by William de Rubruquis a few decades earlier:

The people [of Samara] have no wheat, but live on rice. Nor have they any wine except such as I shall now describe.

You must know that they derive it from a certain kind of tree that they have. When they want wine they cut a branch of this, and attach a great pot to the stem of the tree at the place where the branch was cut; in a day and a night they will find the pot filled. This wine is an excellent drink, and is got both white and red. It is of such surpassing virtue that it cures dropsy and tisick and spleen. The trees resemble small date palms;... and when cutting a branch no longer gives a flow of wine, they water the root of the tree, and before long the branches again begin to give out wine as before.

Indonesia is still famed for Batavia arrack, a distillate of fermented sugar cane juice and red rice (aka: weedy rice). What Polo encountered was a style of arrack made from sugar palm juice that is indigenous to western Indonesia. In annotated translations of Polo's work by Henry Yule (1903) and Henri Cordier (1920), the specific type of sugar palm Polo referred to is called the *Areng Saccharifera*. It is also called *gomuti* in Malaysia and *saguer* by the Portuguese.

Dictated to fellow prisoner Rustichello of Pisa while he was imprisoned, in 1298, for his involvement in a military conflict between Venice and Genoa, Polo's

Il Milione, was a massive best seller, translated into numerous European languages even before the invention of the printing press. One of these copies made it into the hands of a Portuguese prince, triggering the invention of three New World spirits. But we will get to that story after we talk about the Venetian merchants arch rivals, the trading houses of Genoa.

THE MERCHANTS OF GENOA

While the venetian merchant Marco Polo may have remarked about arrack, the principality's main competitors, the Genoese merchants, were responsible for exporting the spirit to Europe. However, their influence came with a terrible cost.

By the thirteenth century, the Genoese had established a commercial colony at Trebizond, in northern Turkey: an entry point to overland trade with India. A second settlement at Caffa on the Crimean Peninsula secured their stake in imports from China and Indonesia via Muslim traders. Controllers of the spice trade by that time, the Muslims also imported sweet oranges and other exotic treats such as arrack from these far-off lands according to historian Lincoln P Paine. another researcher named David

Arnold found evidence that the Genoese also invested their profits into enterprises in North Africa and the Iberian Peninsula, especially on Madeira, where they imported Asian sugar cane seedlings and established sizable plantations and sugar mills. They cut out the Muslim middlemen and reduced the cost of transport of these commodities to European buyers. This proved to be an exceptionally good investment decades later.

From these pivotal locations, the Genoese plied their wares along the Mediterranean through Cyprus, Egypt, Genoa, Mallorca and by the 1270s, to Bruges in Belgium, initiating the first sustained navigation between Mediterranean and Atlantic seaports. Conflict between the Ottoman and Mongol empires as well as with the Venetians made trade increasingly difficult. In an attempt to circumvent their Muslim middlemen as well as to avoid clashes with Egyptian Mamluks and the Mongols, the Genoese ventured out into the Atlantic in search of alternate sea routes.

In his 1996 book *Genoa and the Genoese: 958–1528*, author Steven A Epstein mentions that in the spring of

1291, Ugolino and Vadino Vivaldi set sail from Genoa via Ceuta in Spain onward to the Atlantic in hopes of reaching India. They never returned home: their story became part of Genoese sea lore, and quite possibly inspiration to Christopher Columbus, who was later born in the great trading capital.

Despite the political and business upheavals merchants stationed in Caffa and Trebizond were fortunate. They did not experience the seven-year-long famine (1314–1321) that devastated most of Europe. They were never affected by the typhoid and anthrax epidemics that came in its wake. Although the very real fear of infected water increased interest and demand for arrack as a base for making medicine and as an anaesthetic – of which, the Genoese were major purveyors – the market came to a quick halt because of something else they unintentionally imported.

In his 2004 book *The Black Death: 1346–1353*, Ole Jørgen Benedictow postulates that the bubonic plague originated in the steppes of Central Asia or in northern India. But around 1335, the plague swept west across China, transported by the caravans along the Silk Road. The disease reached epidemic proportions, by November, 1346, devastating the vast Mongol empire from Beijing to the Caucasus. In their 1987 *Cambridge Economic History of Europe*, historians MM Postan and Edward Miller relate that in the winter of that year, Kipchuk Khan Janibeg led his plague-infected army of Tartars and Mongols to the Crimea. The khan laid siege to Caffa, the following spring, despite the fact his men were dying by the scores. Possibly as an act of desperation, the khan deployed a lethal biological weapon: He ordered his surviving troops to catapult their dead over the city walls.

Panicked Genoese fled. Their ships carried the pathogen agents with them: infected survivors of the siege, black rats and their fleas. Their exodus, by sea and by land, left every port of call victim to the Black Death. By May 1347, the Byzantine capital of Constantinople was contaminated; Trebizond fell by late summer. Then in October, a handful of refugee ships landed in Messina, Sicily. Most of the crew and passengers were either dead or dying. Other ships ran aground, brimming with infected corpses. By the spring of 1348, the plague ravaged both Genoa and Venice before it encompassed the rest of Europe, killing somewhere between one third and one half of its population. By 1351, the toll also included half of Asia and one eighth of Africa.

Three decades later, the Genoese merchants were back in business. They lost their interests in the spice trade after they were defeated by their longtime foes, the Venetians, in the 1381 War of Chiogga. But they continued their investment in the Iberian sugar trade and pursued the interests they had established in Poland.

During the 1100s, the Genoese merchants had established strong relations with the papal tax-collectors connected to the Florentine banking houses, thus gaining access to goods from the north and east such as copper, fur and leather which they exchanged for fine textiles, fruits, wines and sugar. Two centuries later, they took on an additional job becoming money movers. Taxes collected from Poland on behalf of the Vatican were shipped from Krakow through Wroclaw to their trading port at Bruges and then on to Italy.

The Genoese opened new routes to the Black Sea and delved into other ventures. They leased the royal salt mines in Bochema and Wieliczka. They invested in lead mines in Olkusz and Tzrebinia. One entrepreneur Goffredo Fattinanti leased and operated the royal mint, then permanently settled in Krakow. The influx of Genoese including Cristoforo de S. Romolo, Lorenzo Lomellino and the De Veletariis family into Poland and then into southern-Russia continued well into the fifteenth century.

By this time, word of potable distillates reached far beyond the Iberian Peninsula, Catalonia and southern France in the west and in Germany to the northeast. Hailed as an excellent vehicle for preserving the potency of treatments for many ailments, alcohol was also gaining interest as a pleasurable beverage. Using their Spanish sugar cane supplies, the Genoese launched into arrack production. Once again, they cut out the expense of transport and the Muslim middlemen.

William Pokhlebkin in the 1992 English translation of his book, *A History of Vodka*, noted there was no "definite indication of the starting material for distillation", postulating that the Genoese possessed grape wine and "obtained their knowledge of distillation from the Provençals, who used grape wine." But a grape brandy would not have

had half the market allure that a sugar-based spirit would have among affluent consumers who revelled in exotic Asian goods.

It is very probable that the liquor produced and traded in Poland and Russia was made from sugar cane juice and marketed either as arrack or as *aqua vitae*. Why? Because grappa – brandy made by distilling the pomace (grape skins, stems and seeds left over from wine production) – was a speciality of the Veneto region of Italy. Why make a product that brought the Venetians any notoriety? Why not exploit a well-seated investment in sugar? Why not capitalize on the success of Marco Polo's memoirs and its mention of sugar-based spirit?

Pokhlebkin also implied that in 1386 Genoese emissaries may have presented samples of *aqua vitae* to Russian Grand Prince Dmitri Ivanovich Donskoi on their way to Lithuania via Moscow. They may very well have imported the spirit and the technology to Poland for personal consumption and for trade. Whether it was arrack or some other form of spirit, it is certain that the Genoese were key protagonists in convincing Poland and Russia to develop their own spirits. According to one source, the sampling was a success. The Polish Vodka Association states that the first reference to the spirit appeared in the 1405 court records of the Swietokrzyskie Voivodship. We have not found the actual document, but we did see a 1534 text in Warsaw that referred to it.

When the Geneose passed through Russia again, in 1426, historian Pokhlebkin tells us that Grand Prince Vasily the Third Vassilievitch was more than delighted to receive a bottle of their spirit. Within a few years, monasteries were ordered to produce a grain-based version called "bread wine."

A couple of decades later, time and technology converged with demand to create and explosion of spirits.

THE SPREAD OF SPIRITS

Within a century, all of the research and work of al-Jabir, al-Kindi, al-Razi, de Ville-Neuve, Llull, Bacon and Magnus manifested itself into a commercial enterprise. According to historian Frederick H Smith, De Ville-Neuve's brandy recipe left the confines of the apothecary and was in full-scale production throughout the Armagnac region by 1411, registered

as a commercial product three years later in Saint-Sever. Similar step-ups in production and popularity occurred in Ireland, Poland, Russia and Scotland.

For the first half of the fifteenth century, the transfer of information was slow. It took time to hand-copy each of the treatises. The expense of hiring professional scribes was prohibitive for even the most affluent noble. That is, until Johannes Gutenberg unveiled his system for mass-producing movable type and his printing press in 1450. The subsequent information explosion ignited the nascent alcohol industry.

One of the first authors to take advantage of this new technology was Viennese physician Michael Puff von Schrick, who wrote a description of 82 herbal liquors entitled *A Very Useful Little Book on Distillations* in 1455, revising it in 1466. The book was printed and published in 38 editions, beginning in 1476. The last edition came off the press in 1601.

Bacon, Llull and Magnus were posthumously best-selling authors as was de Ville-Neuve, whose *Liber de Vinis* was translated into English and published in 1478.

Thanks to this information avalanche, other nations joined in producing unique eaux-de-vie. In Germany, kirschwasser (a cherry eau-de-vie predominantly produced from morello cherries) became an overnight success. The printing press also helped to disseminate cautions about overindulgence. In 1493, a physician in Nuremburg wrote:

> *In view of the fact that everyone at present has got into the habit of drinking aqua vitae it is necessary to remember the quantity that one can permit oneself to drink and learn to drink it according to one's capacities, if one wishes to behave like a gentleman.*

Few took heed.

Back in the British Isles, Scottish production of *aqua vitae* – called *uisge-beatha* [whisky] – accelerated. In 1494, an entry in the Exchequer Rolls listed:

> *To Friar John Cor, by order of the King [James IV], to make aqua vitae VIII bolls of malt."*

Four years later, the Lord High Treasurer's Account recorded payment:

> *To the barbour that brocht aqua vitae to the King in Dundee.*

Since barbers served as physicians as well as hair trimmers, it stands to reason distilling secrets would have passed from the monastery to the barbershop. By 1505, a monopoly to produce spirits was granted in Edinburgh to the newly chartered Guild of Surgeons and Barbers to produce spirits.

Printing presses and books proliferated in every European country. One major work was Hieronymus Brunschweig's 1500 title, *Liber de arte distillandi; Das buch der rechten kunst zu distillieren* [Book of the Distillation Art: A book on the right way to distil], which was published in Strasbourg. The book inspired the establishment of numerous distilling houses in neighbouring Schiedam and Amsterdam that produced *brandewijn* [burnt wine] from malted grain.

Polish pharmacist Stefan Falimirz's 1534 book of medical treatments *O Ziolach I O Mocy Ich* detailed the preparation of over 70 vodka-based medicines: the first document to use the term "wodka". The book detailed the employment of an alembic for rectification of this spirit with herbs, such as borage and centaury. It also put forth recommendations on the smoking of vodka with alder or other aromatic woods.

Back in western distillation's home country, France, King Louis XII licenced vinegar producers, in 1514, to make eaux-de-vie. King Francis I allowed wholesale grocers to produce spirits in 1537. Then French distillers organized, in the mid-1550s, into a separate guild.

The monasteries that for centuries translated and hand-copied distillation treatises also entered the playing field as spirits producers. In 1510, Bénédictine monk Dom Bernardo Vincelli created an herbal eau-de-vie at the Abbey of Fécamp, which to this day bears the name Bénédictine. When Catherine de Medici married King Henry II of France, she brought with her cooks to make her favourite delicacies from her native Tuscany as well as bottles of Liquore Mediceo, Fraticello and Elixir Stomatico di Lunga Vita, which were specialities produced in the mountain-top monasteries surrounding Florence.

These early decades of the 1500s also saw the birth of the New World spirits. Not the result of accident or spontaneous discovery, these libations were born from massive shifts in Europe's political and economic arenas.

CHAPTER FIVE
The Atlantic Passage

NEW WORLD SPIRITS & THE AGE OF CONQUEST

The fifteenth century was a period of rampant economic competition and national imperialism in Europe. The rulers of Spain, Britain, France and Portugal were more than envious of the Italian city-states' monopolies on Asian trade. No one wanted to lose a stake in the bounty that lay just within reach.

Ships were built. Navigators trained. Ambitious sea voyages were funded in hopes of finding alternate water routes to India and China. To gain approval of their actions, Christian monarchs sought papal benediction for their plans. They cited these explorations as excellent opportunities to spread Christianity to the far corners of the known world as well as ideal way to stem the growth of Muslim influence.

THE RACE BEGINS

Originally commissioned by Charles V of France, in 1375, the Catalan Atlas was supposedly drawn by Jahuda Cresques of Barcelona: the first chart to give a fairly accurate rendering of Ceylon and the Indian Peninsula, as well as the west coast of Africa to Cape Bojador. The nautical data was based on the pilot books of various vessels and records show that much of Marco Polo's information aided in the drawing of the land portions.

The Catalan Atlas of World was as important a reference tool as Marco Polo's *Il Milione* to one particular monarch, Portugal's Prince Henrique O Navegador (Henry the Navigator; 1390–1464). No ruler was more successful than Henrique at casting his net into the uncharted waters of the Atlantic. No ruler did as much to launch the race to find the Atlantic passage to the Orient.

Founder of Europe's first school of navigation, Henrique educated and sponsored explorers who, in 1427, sailed south from Gibraltar down the coast of Mauretania to the Azores. By 1444, Portuguese explorers reached Cabo Verde in Senegal.

At each landfall, Henrique's explorers established trade and built settlements on land leased from local rulers. By the time Henrique died, Portugal claimed the Cape Verde Islands south of the Spanish-held Canary Islands, a point further than any European had ever reached.

Spain was also extending its interests beyond the western and southern borders of Europe in its search for alternate routes to Asia. To keep future peace between these two Christian kingdoms, Pope Sixtus IV issued Papal Bull *Aeterni regis* [Eternally Rule], in 1481, granting Portugal rights to all land south of the Canary Islands, from both east to west. This also reinforced Spain's ownership of the Canaries themselves.

Portugal advanced its claims, by 1471, as far south as the Gold Coast (now known as Ghana). Then it set its sights on securing a direct sea route to Asia via Africa's southern tip. Explorer and navigator Bartolomeo Diaz accomplished the first half of this feat in 1487, sailing south and claiming the Cape of Good Hope in the name of Portugal before he was forced to return home to avoid mutiny by his crew.

Spain leapt ahead with the successful 1492 voyage of Genoese navigator Christopher Columbus, who sailed under a Spanish flag. Another Papal Bull *Inter caetera* [Among the Rest] issued by Pope Alexander VI on 4 May 1493, reset the ownership boundaries, granting Spain all lands west and south of a pole-to-pole line positioned one hundred leagues from the Cape Verde Islands. This demarcation was much looser than a specific point of measurement, an island in the cluster or a degree of longitude. Naturally, Spain was pleased. Portugal was not.

On 7 June 1494, Pope Alexander VI drafted the Treaty of Tordesilhas, which gave Portugal carte blanche to claim any lands discovered between the Portuguese Cape Verde Islands and the islands of San Salvador in the Bahamas, Cuba and Hispaniola (claimed by Spain). Appeased by this decision, Portugal continued the conquest of the Atlantic Passage.

THE LAND OF THE TRUE CROSS

Commissioned by King Manuel I of Portugal and additionally funded by a group of Florentine merchants, explorer Pedro Álvares Cabral (1467–1520) led a daring expedition, following da Gama's original course. Thirteen ships left Lisbon, in 1500, on a course for the Cape of Good Hope. In his memoirs, *Memória das Armadas que de Portugal passaram à Índia* [Memory of the Portuguese Navies' Passage to India], Cabral recounted that the fleet left harbour on Monday, 9 March. Taking care to avoid the Doldrums [the Intertropical Convergence Zone] off Africa's Gulf of Guinea, they reached the Cape Verde Islands on 22 March.

Fleet captain Pedro Vaz de Caminha recounted that:

On the following night, the Monday, we discovered at dawn that Vasca de Ataíde and his ship had been lost, though there was no strong or contrary wind to account for this [He later rejoined them]. The admiral [Cabral] sought him diligently in all directions, but he did not appear again. So we continued on our way across the ocean on the Tuesday of Easter week, which was 21st April, we came across some signs of being near land, at some 660 or 670 leagues from the aforesaid island by the pilot's computation. ...On the following morning, Wednesday,...at the hour of vespers we sighted land, that is to say, first a very high mountain, then other lower ranges of hills to the south of it, and a plain covered with large trees. The admiral named the mountain

Easter Mount and the country the Land of the True Cross.

With that, claim was made on what would eventually be called Brazil. Leaving a handful of settlers on the "island", Cabral resumed his voyage to India on 3 May, reaching the Cape of Good Hope at the end of the month.

SIMPLE LUXURIES

Necessity has always bred invention. And the birth of the New World Spirits was no exception. Within the brief 30-year span in which the Spanish and Portuguese discovered, conquered and colonized the New World, three spirit categories emerged. Their births trace back to the prohibitive cost and difficulty of importing a regular supply of *bagaceira* [brandy] from Portugal or brandy from Spain.

Throughout history, there has never been significant period of time when humankind has not discovered, developed and consumed fermented beverages for religious, medical or social purposes. The New World was no exception. Before European settlement, the indigenous peoples of the Caribbean as well as Central and South America produced fermented beverages, used for religious purposes just as India's Proto-Indo-Iranians and Hindus imbibed *somasara*.

Mesoamerican Toltec, Aztec and Olmec legends abound about the birth of maguey – the blue Weber agave or century plant – and the fermented beverage pulque or octli. Purportedly a gift from the gods, the beverage was fermented *aguamiel* [honey water] extracted from maguey, the most sacred plant in their religious traditions. Aztec priests fashioned lightning bolt sceptres from maguey leaves, which they used in blood-letting rituals.

Historian Frederick H Smith tells us that the Taínos (aka: Arawaks) of the Bahamas and Greater Antilles as well as the Caribs of the Lesser Antilles consumed a beverage fermented from manioc, called perino or oüicuo by the Caribs or made from yams called mobbie.

The Tupinambá of Brazil drank similar beverages. Cauim was made from manioc (aka: yucca, cassava) and avati was made from millet. Both were cooked, chewed and spat out by women and then re-cooked to break down the starch into fermentable sugar. This method is not dissimilar to the process employed

by the Japanese in the making of the earliest-known form of sake, *kuchikami no sake* [chewing the mouth alcoholic beverage]. Jean de Léry described the process in the 1550s in his *History of a Voyage to the Land of Brazil*:

These roots, aypi and maniot, serve as their chief nourishment, prepared in the way that I have described; now here is how they handle them to make their customary drink.

After the women have cut up the roots as fine as we cut turnips for stewing, they let the pieces boil in water in great earthen vessels; when they see them getting tender and soft, they remove the pots from the fire and let them cool a little. When that is done, several of the women, crouched around these great vessels, take from them little round pieces of softened root. First they chew them and twist them around in their mouths without swallowing them; then they take the pieces in their hands, one after the other and put them into other earthen vessels which are already on the fire, and in which they boil the pieces again. They constantly stir this concoction with a stick until they see that it is done, and then removing it from the fire a second time without straining it, they pour it all into other bigger earthen jars, each having the capacity of about an eleven-gallon Burgundy wine-measure. After it has clarified and fermented, they cover the vessels and leave the beverage until people want to drink it, in the manner that I will, shortly describe.

THE PLACE OF HARVESTING PLANTS

One of the first spirits to be divined from European encounters with New World natives was mezcal, the mother of tequila.

According to Aztec myth, the god of healing and fertility, Quetzalcoatl, eloped with the goddess of fertility Mayahuel, descending to Earth. When Mayahuel's grandmother realized the girl had runaway, she sent the *tzitzimime* [star demons] to hunt her down.

Quetzacoatl and Mayahuel tried to disguise themselves as the branches of a tree. But the *tzitzimime* found them and the tree split in two. Recognizing the branch that bore Mayahuel, her enraged grandmother shredded it apart and gave the *tzitzimime* pieces of her to eat. Quetzalcoatl was unharmed. When they left, the bereft deity returned to his usual form. He buried what was left of Mayahuel's remains. From that grave sprouted the first maguey plants.

The neighbouring Nahuatls also believed the maguey was divine, personified by Mayahuel, who was depicted as a goddess with 400 breasts that oozed pulque. Her 400 children who were nurtured on pulque represented the numerous forms that intoxication takes in the human body: a cornucopia of altered states that freed the soul.

When the Spanish conquistadors arrived in the New World in 1521, they learned of pulque as they ravaged and conquered the Aztec, Toltec and Olmec worlds. The conquerors moved north and west until, in 1530, the Teochinchenses people surrendered to the conquistador Cristóbal de Oñate (1504–1567) after numerous bloody battles and handed over control of Chiquihuitillo Hill.

Oñate established the village of Santiago de Tequila on the hill and appointed Juan de Escarcena to oversee its settlement. At one point, Oñate reported to Spain's King Carlos I about the products the natives obtained from the local agaves: "From these plants they make wine and sugar, which they also sell."

It was nearly impossible to import brandy to this far western outpost. So when the supplies ran out the Spanish found a solution. The following year, they constructed *alquitaras* (alembic stills made from mud, wood, a pot and a basin) in a nearby ravine and distilled brandy from pulque.

Archaeological evidence found in Colima and Jalisco points to another introduction of distillation to the area. Filipino seamen sailing on galleons from Manila also brought stills with them when they arrived on the northwest Mexico coast during the 1530s, which they used to make lambanog, a coconut-based arrack. According to some researchers, when the coconuts ran out, the seamen also resorted to distilling fermented agave.

Whether the technology was first imported by the Filipinos or the Spanish, the end result was the same. The distillate that became known as mexcalli was pleasant to drink. Fray Toribiode Benavente "Motolinía" commented, in 1541, that:

> ...from this genus of metl...comes out better that wine which I have said some Spaniards drink and I have drunk it...this they cook underground; the leaf fronds by themselves, or the heads by themselves...and thus call it mexcalli; but if the heads are cooked by a good master, and in those places

that are better than others, it has good tajadas, which many Spaniards desire as much as dyacitron. If anyone asks if there exist many of these metl, I say that all the land is full of them.

The progression from successful experiment to commercial production took less than seventy-five years. Around 1600, Don Pedro Sánchez de Tagle, the Marquis of Altamira, established the first commercial production of the agave spirit and eight years later the colonial governor of Nueva Galicia imposed a tax on his growing inventory.

SWEETNESS TO LIFE

The story of cachaça's birth follows a similar theme. After the discovery of Brazil, in 1500, it was 30 years before the royal court felt obliged to protect its new resources. Remember: at the time, Portugal's main interest was Asia. The discovery of another "island" in the unknown New World meant little to a king who needed to pay off his war debts and refill his coffers. However, one item did draw his interest: the island's abundance of pau-Brazil (aka: Brazilwood). Imported from Asia in powdered form, this red dye was a prized possession amongst European nobility who a penchant for wearing deep red garments. The discovery of this same tree proliferating on the newly claimed island was an unexpected treat.

It took only a few years before a crown-granted Portuguese monopoly was established. It took no time for British pirates and French corsairs to attack Portuguese ships, hoping to capture this precious cargo. And it took even less time for British and French profiteers to harvest and smuggle the wood as contraband along the southern coast, especially in the captaincy of São Vicente.

Pillage of the Brazilian forests continued unabated until the monarchy finally decided to colonise Brazil. The Spanish conquest of Mesoamerica was his wake-up call. King John III of Portugal, in 1530, sent Martim Afonso de Sousa to Brazil with a fleet of noble-born captains to explore and establish settlements. Because of de Sousa's efforts, the monarch awarded each captaincy one to three regions to develop and exploit in the name of the Portuguese crown.

De Sousa and his captains established sugar cane plantations along the coast from north to south. According to historian Marcelo Cámara, in 1533, Martim Afonso de Sousa and

his partners Pero Lopes de Sousa, Francisco Lobo, Vicente Gonçalves and Erasmo Shetz of Antwerp not only set up three sugar mills at São Jorge dos Erasmos, Madre de Deus and São João, they installed copper alembics to distil *garapa azeda* [sugar cane wine] into *aguardente de caña* [sugar cane eau-de-vie], which was later called cachaça, the second New World spirit.

The idea of colonists such as de Sousa and the Spanish conquistadors importing alembics as a basic piece of equipment is not as bizarre as one would initially think. Settling in the barbaric New World demanded the importation of every essential for survival. Transporting an alembic meant that medicines as well as potable alcohol were available. A printed distillation book and an abundant supply of raw material made the process of making cane spirit as easy as baking a cake.

There was a ready market for cachaça. As maritime commerce in Brazilian sugar and other products intensified, and as the settlement population increased, the number of New World distilleries blossomed. Between 1585 and 1629, the number of Brazilian cachaça distilleries alone rose from 192 to 349.

The Portuguese poet Francisco de Sá de Miranda (1481–1558) was an early fan of cachaça. The brother of Mem de Sá (Brazil's third governor-general, from 1557 to 1572) and a friend to King John III and the royal court, Sá de Miranda was held in high regard for introducing the sonnet, the elegy and the ecologue as poetic forms to the Portuguese language. He was also famed for his letters, which were written entirely in verse. Living on the Quinta da Tapada estate owned by Antônio Pereira, the poet first sampled a cask of cachaça (probably a gift from his brother) and wrote the following verse in a letter to his landlord:

Ali, não mordia a graça,
Eram iguais os juizes,
Não vinha nada da praça,
Ali, da vossa cachaça!
Ali, das vossas perdizes!

[There, it did not bite to grace,
They were equal the judges
Comes nothing of the plaza,
There, of your cachaça!
There, of your partridges!]

This is one of the first documented uses of the word "cachaça." Before then, the spirit was commonly referred to as *grappa*, *aguardente* [burning water] or *bagaceira* [brandy]. It remained a pleasant curiosity for the nobility for a few centuries.

TO THE FARTHEST REACHES

Spanish colonists in Peru had an even harder time than their Central American and Caribbean colleagues importing brandy and other small luxuries from home. And wine was nearly impossible to acquire and preserve. The first Peruvian vineyards were planted, in 1533, by Marquis Francisco de Caravantes, who imported the grape stock from the Canary Islands.

His hunch about the soil and climate met with success. Within five years, Spanish settlers harvested and exported their New World wine. Grape harvests that were not deemed suitable for export were discarded or their must was given to tenant farmers. It is believed that was the birth of pisco: the farmers made a grape eau-de-vie or *aguardiente* from the must because it was more economical than importing brandy.

Pisco distillation must have also thrived like mezcal and cachaça. In 1613, a resident of the town of Pisco named Pedro Manuel the Greek listed among his possessions in his last will and testament 30 containers plus one barrel of "grape brandy", a large copper pot and the essential utensils needed to produce pisco.

RICH MAN, POOR MAN

Since the importation of bagaceira, pomace brandy, port and other potable beverages from the motherlands cost a fortune in shipping and exportation tax, it is not surprising that these explorers and colonists who regarded Marco Polo as a role model were eager to produce a "local spirit" that allowed them to sustain their upper-class European lifestyle.

What of the association between sugar cane workers – who were mostly slaves and indentured indigenous people – and these new spirits? Little to none. Their drink was cagaça, which was a simple sugar cane wine substitute for the Tupis' beer-strength, manioc-based cauim, the Caribs' perino and West African akpeteshi or burukutu [date-palm wine]. None of these were distilled spirits.

Economic segregation of beverages was common around the world. During the fifteenth and sixteenth centuries vodka, whiskey and eau-de-vies were the beverages of choice at the royal courts of Poland, Russia, Britain, Ireland, Germany, France and Italy. But the commoners, the peasants, the servants drank beer and mead.

Alembics were costly to build, own and operate. They required technical skill and scientific knowledge: an education and literacy were needed to make spirits. Fermentation, on the other hand, was cheap and easy. Put the liquid out to collect air-borne wild yeast and wait a few days. Consequently, it stands to reason that cachaça, mezcal and pisco were the beverages of the colonial upper classes while cagaça, perino, pulque, cauim and burukutu were the drinks of the indigenous people, imported slaves and indentured servants.

EL DRAQUE: THE FIRST MOJITO

One of the earliest mixed drinks to use a New World spirit as its feature ingredient was invented for a British privateer. Despite what some historians relate, the drink was not originally made with rum, it was made with cachaça.

When British adventurer Sir Francis Drake (1540–1596) made his first voyage to the Caribbean in 1563, he was a slave trader, hauling human cargo from Africa on board his cousin John Hawkins' ship. He took an immediate dislike to the Spanish and they reciprocated his feelings. Things got worse in 1568. His ship was ambushed by the Spanish fleet while delivering another load of slaves. Surviving only because he knew how to swim, Drake devoted his life to wreaking revenge on the Spanish Empire. The Spanish labelled him a pirate, the British called him a privateer and Britain's Queen Elizabeth I privately declared him to be one of her court favourites. The Spanish dubbed him "El Draque" [the Dragon].

During the 1570s, Drake and his crew of French sailors and Cimarrones (aka: Maroons) – African slaves who escaped from sugar plantations – took up privateering as a profession. It was a "legitimized" form of piracy. Wealthy businessmen and nobles financed privateers' escapades for a share in the loot.

Some stories say that pirate Richard Drake invented a drink that he named after his boss, El Draque. The basic concoction included readily available ingredients from a pirate's point of view: sugar, key limes, spirit and a variety of local mint known locally as *hierba buena* which grew naturally in and around sugar cane fields. (The mint was a mild form with a red-hued stem: *Mentha suaveolens*, which is also known as apple mint, woolly mint or Cuban mint.)

How did this Drake divine such a concoction? Drake's Cimarron crew members not only knew of cachaça, but knew the location of the northern Brazilian distilleries situated along the coast.

How do we know that this is the true provenance of the drink? If the story of the El Draque is true, it had to be made with cachaça. Drake died in 1596 and rum was developed four decades later. Cuban rum historian Fernando Campoamor uncovered that fact in this tale. El Draque was given this potion as a remedy to settle his stomach, which was affected by the tropical climate and diet. Centuries after El Draque's death, Drakes or Draquecitos were still taken by Caribbean settlers as a refreshing break to the day. Cuban author Ramon de Palma noted this in his 1838 story *El Cólera en Habana* when he wrote: "I take every day at eleven o'clock a Draquecito and its does me perfectly."

When did the Draquecito evolve into the Mojito? According to author Ciro Bianchi Ross and historian Miguel Bonera, the Mojito Batido first appeared in print around 1910 and was served at La Concha in Havana. By that time, commercial ice had been imported and then produced in the city for nearly a hundred years. Havana's cantineros relished serving icy cold drinks. Muddling the fragrant mint, adding crystal clear ice and topping it with soda water transformed the El Draque into a refreshment deserving a name of special merit.

Many of Havana's finest hotels and bars embraced the Mojito in the first decades of the twentieth century. But it was the hands of Angel Martinez at La Bodeguita del Medio and celebrity promotion by novelist Ernest Hemingway shaped the drink into an international legend.

DUTCH COURAGE

Juniper berries were regarded as an ideal antiseptic, diuretic, antiviral and detoxifier since Greek and Roman times. Sixteenth-century Europeans also inherited a taste for them. Gathered from an evergreen shrub, these pungent berries were a potent preventative against disease. Following in the path of Hippocrates, herbalists and alchemists placed a few juniper berries in their mouths or in masks to serve as an antiseptic barrier between them and their patients. They even steeped the berries in water and used the tea a disinfectant for needles and bandages.

The earliest recorded infusion of juniper into spirit took place in Italy. Opened in the ninth century, the medical school in Salerno, Italy, was espousing the benefits of juniper elixir by 1055. Their *Compendium Salerni* medical book contained the earliest European reference to distilled spirit, which they called *aqua ardens* [burning water].

When the Black Death raged across the Continent and the British Isles (1347–1350), people burned juniper incense, wore masks laced with juniper oil and filled with juniper berries and consumed juniper elixirs in hopes of warding off the plague. In truth, though they did not know it at the time, they had found a mildly effective preventative. The host for the bubonic plague pathogen is a parasite carried by a flea that is particularly attracted to black rats. Juniper is an excellent flea repellent.

To combat disease in general, juniper was also employed as a flavouring and preservative in smoked meats, sausages, stews and other foods. By the sixteenth century, its appeal had broadened from valuable medicine to a preferred flavour.

According to jenever historian Philip Duff, juniper-based health tonics and medicines were first mentioned in Jacob van Maerlant te Damme's 1269 book, *Der Naturen Bloeme* [Of the Nature Flower]. But a juniper eau-de-vie did not make its appearance until 1552, when Philippus Hermanni referred to a juniper-infused distillate in his book *Constelijck Distilleer Boek* [Constelijck Distiller Book]. Many Dutch distillers (known as *coornbranders*) tested numerous recipes that incorporated this pungent berry. Junpier's woodsy aroma and hops-laced flavour masked any unpleasant odours in their unfiltered, unrefined *korenbrandewijn* that was distilled from roasted barley malt and other grains.

Some sources say that a sweet juniper eau-de-vie called "genever" was produced in Geneva, Switzerland. But closer to the truth is that *eau-de-vie de genièvre* translates from the French to juniper brandy. Crossing the border to Flanders, the word was transposed to "genever." Arriving in the Netherlands, it became "jenever."

However one person seemed to receive the most notoriety for his formula, at least from a historical perspective: Dr Sylvius de Bouve from the University of Leyden. No, not Dr Franciscus de la Böe (1614–1672), who was many years de Bouve's junior and was also known as Dr Sylvius. The younger Dr Sylvius focused on the structure of the brain and discovered the cleft now known as Sylvian fissure. Sylvius de Bouve concentrated on pharmaceuticals and the digestive tract.

Many writers have echoed this mistaken identity since the 1800s when the two Dr Sylviuses from the University of Leyden were erroneously assumed to be the same person. (We also previously believed Franciscus le Böe was the creator of jenever. Then we uncovered the truth, thanks to Mr Duff.)

Sylvius de Bouve (aka: Franciscus Sylvius) was a well-known pharmacist, chemist and alchemist during the sixteenth century. He experimented with rectifying *korenbrandwijn* with juniper berries for their medicinal benefits: an ideal treatment for lumbago as well as similar aches and pains. De Bouve began selling his creation, by 1595, under the brand name "Genova."

Twenty years earlier, Lucas Bulsius and his family had moved to Amsterdam from Cologne via Flanders. Bulsius learned how to distil spirits in Cologne and hoped to set up his own operation in his new home. That is when the family name changed to Bols.

Fortune smiled upon Bols. By 1602, he was a preferred supplier to the Seventeen Gentlemen, the inner circle of the powerful Dutch East India Company. He got first dibs on cargos of herbs and spices, which gave him an advantage when making his particular recipe of jenever. In return, the Dutch East India Company crewmen and officers received daily rations of the spirit in a measured pewter cup that marked the mandatory daily issue of one half pint.

Lucas Bols' establishment, in 1575, was one of 200 distillation houses that had quickly cropped up to make juniper tonics. Thus, jenever was available by the late 1580s when British troops first landed in the Netherlands to fight the Spanish during the Dutch War of Independence (1567–1609). According to historian Alan S Dikty, the British gratefully drank drams of it to give them "Dutch courage" during battle. The troops that came to fight during the Thirty Years War (1618-48) similarly found their nerve drinking jenever and happily brought home their taste for what they called "gin".

Following his ascent to the throne, in 1688, Britain's new Dutch king, William of Orange (1650–1702), fostered the importation of jenever, restricted French brandy imports and, most importantly, encouraged his British subjects to distil "good English corn" into gin. The London Guild of Distillers was soon disbanded, opening the way for gin distillation by amateurs. Two years later, Londoners gin production and consumption rose to 500,000 gallons per annum.

Daniel Defoe, author of the novel *Robinson Crusoe*, lauded King William's edict, writing in the 1713 Review that:

Nothing is more certain than the fact that the ordinary production of grain in England is much greater than our people or cattle can consume. Because gin is made from grain, the distilling trade is one remedy for this disaster as it helps to carry off the great quantity of grain in such a time of plenty. In times of plenty and a moderate price of grain, the distilling of grain is one of the most essential things to support the landed interest and therefore especially to be preserved.

It was duly noted in the 1721 Excise Revenue Accounts that approximately one quarter of London's habitable structures were employed in the production and sales of nearly 2,000,000 gallons (or 840,000 nine-litre cases) of tax-free gin. Between the 1720s and 1730s, nearly 7,000 gin shops offered the city's staggering half-million population a place to imbibe a dram of gin for no more than a penny per serving. As Jessica Warner wrote in her 2002 book, *Craze: Gin and Debauchery in an Age of Reason*:

In 1700, the average adult drank slightly more than a third of a gallon of cheap spirits over the course of a year; by 1720 that amount had nearly doubled; and by 1729, the year when the first Act restricting sales of gin was passed, the number had nearly doubled again, to slightly more than 1.3 gallons [about 5 litres] per person. The figures included only the population fifteen years of age or older, although there were as yet no formal restrictions on minors' access to alcohol.

Legal and illegal gin production rampaged as the major cities fell into a well-documented mass drunken stupor. Gin was the drink of the unemployed and the under-paid who toiled while their employers made fortunes on paper in the South Sea Bubble. It was the drink of the poor, who never got a break even before the Bubble burst and plunged England into an economic depression.

Idle time and excess gin were an unhealthy combination, and public outcry for temperance and prohibition were immortalized in pamphlets such as *Distilled Liquors: the Bane of the Nation* (1736), which reported that:

Everyone who now passes through the streets of the great city of London and looks into the gin shops must see, even in shops of creditable and wholesome appearance, a crowd of poor ragged people, cursing and quarreling with one another over repeated glasses of these destructive liquors. In one place not far from East Smithfield, a trader has a large empty room where, as his wretched guests get intoxicated, they are laid together in heaps, men, women and children, until they recover their senses, when they proceed to drink on, or having spent all they had, go out to find the means to return to the same dreadful pursuit.

But the British Parliament viewed gin production as an economic essential not a public hazard. As the First Earl of Bath, William Pulteney, said in a 1736 speech to Parliament:

Let us consider, Sir, that the gin trade has been carried on for about 100 years and that it has been very much encouraged by several acts of Parliament. No one could imagine that the trade is in itself detrimental to the health and welfare of the people. Accordingly, great numbers of his Majesty's subjects, especially within the last forty years, have entered this business. There is not an inn, an alehouse, or a coffeehouse in the kingdom, but what owes a great part of its profits to the sale of gin. There are now multitudes of families in the kingdom who owe their chief if not their only support to the distilling, or to the sale of such liquor. They deserve the care and the consideration of the British House of Common. I cannot give my consent to any regulation which will put them out of the business to which they owe their chief support.

When the first – and wholly ineffectual – Gin Act of 1736 was passed by Parliament riots broke out across the nation. In the drinking hubs of London, Bristol and Plymouth, mock funeral processions mourned the death of Madame Geneva. (By this time, Britain had six established gin-production centres: London, Bristol, Norwich, Warrington, Liverpool and Plymouth.)

The legislation imposed an excise tax of 20 shillings per gallon on retail sales of gin and required retailers to purchase a £50 annual sales licence. This put legal retailers out of business and stimulated an unbelievable 94 percent rise in consumption and the opening of a staggering number of illegal gin shops. A second act was passed in 1743 that eliminated the excise tax and reduced the licence fee to £1. Domestic consumption reached, in 1743, an all-time high of 2.2 gallons (about 8 litres) per person.

With the passage of the Gin Act of 1751 [aka: the Tippling Act], the 30-year-long "gin epidemic" ended, the tidal wave of cheap spirits receded. This third legislation reduced the license fee to £2 per annum, raised the excise tax to 2.5 shillings per gallon. But it also prohibited gin distillers from directly selling their products or distributing them through unlicenced retailers. The law also restricted retail licences to merchants with substantial property holdings. It was the end of the small gin shops and street sellers.

Consumption sank, the next year, to 1.2 gallons (about 4.5 litres) per person. Limitations on who could produce

and sell gin were then set in place. Combined with new excise taxes on the spirit, the limitations dropped per capita consumption to 0.6 gallons (2.27 litres). However, even this came too late for an estimated 9,000 children in London who died of alcohol poisoning that year.

Enough legislation had been set in place and enforced by the 1790s that the days of cheap gin were finally over. Ironically, these measures which were meant to quash production also caused a dramatic improvement in the quality of British gin. Reputable businessmen took over the gin trade, offering consumers reliable distillates that used more delicate flavourings and less sugar in their formulations than their predecessors, or none at all.

There were a few reasons for this. The first was the invention and implementation of the continuous still, in the 1830s, which improved the quality and quantity of the base spirit. (We'll talk about that later.) The second was the passage of the Excise Act of 1823 (aka: the Wash Act) which imposed an excise tax of 12 pence per 4.5 litres of base spirit produced by distillers. It further imposed a £10 annual licence fee on those distillers. If a firm both distilled

spirits and rectified gin, the overhead was out of reach. Some companies chose to focus on fermentation and distillation. Others chose to rectify gin. The first distiller to formulate and produce a "dry gin", Thomas Coates of Coates & Company in Plymouth made the transition that very year.

A new generation of London gin distillers arose in the years following the Tippling Act and the Excise Act of 1823. Formed in the late 1780s, the Rectifier' Club met at the City of London Tavern in Bishopsgate to discuss matters that affected the business of distilling gin, cordials and other non-whisky spirits made in Britain. Walter and Alfred Gilbey, Seager Evans, Felix Booth, Sir Robert Burnett, Charles Tanqueray, plus Gilbert and John Greenall were all members of this special-interest group which gained prominence during the 1820s.

An early member, Sir Felix Booth (1775–1850) was born into the gin business. His family had founded Booth's Gin in 1740, a decade before the government ended the "Gin Craze." When young Booth joined the company, he did so well with his particular formulation that, in 1829, he financed James Ross's arctic expedition. The Boothia Felix Peninsula in Canada's Northwest Territories was named by Ross as thanks to his benefactor. Three years later, he purchased the site of the old Ophthalmic Hospital on Albany Street in Regent's Park, where he built a larger operation.

James Lys Seager and Williams Evans established, in 1805, their Millbank Distillery near the banks of the River Thames, converting their Seager Evans operations exclusively to gin rectification by 1832.

James Burrough was a relative late-comer to the London rectifier fraternity. John Taylor established a distillery, in 1820, on Cale Street in London's Chelsea district that specialised in making gin and liqueurs. Successful in this venture, Taylor's son joined the business and the company was renamed John Taylor & Son. But the business did not gain its status of being one of the top four nineteenth-century London gin producers until 28-year-old pharmacist James Burrough came into the picture.

Born in Devonshire, Burrough travelled to North America as a young man to train as a pharmacist. While there he also noted the commercial appeal of gin outside of his home country. Returning to London in 1862, Burrough

acquired John Taylor & Son and began distilling Beefeater Gin. He marketed his distinctive dry-style gin, using an image of a Yeoman Warder on the bottle. Of the four London gins of the period, Burrough was the only one to survive and thrive to this day. After a move to Kennington (a few minutes south of Soho) in 1958, the distillery was producing the top selling brand in its category.

Surprised that enterprising people could become that rich from making alcohol? Remember: Every living soul wanted to achieve good health in a world of questionable hygiene and untreated water. So nearly everyone with access to it ingested some form of alcohol every single day. Furthermore, alcohol was a palliative in the century that brought the War of the Spanish Succession, the War of Austrian Succession and the second Jacobite Rebellion. This was also the peak of the Little Ice Age (1400–1850), which ruined crops, triggered monumental storms and blizzards, plunged the world into darkness and generally made the essential task of keeping nourished and warm down right impossible.

Think of it: In a harsh climate in which the global temperature had dropped a mean average of 10 degrees Celsius, a body needed alcohol to wash down corn mush and salted meat after a hard day of lumbering, coopering, shipbuilding, grubbing out the farm, fishing in the North Atlantic or gathering wood to heat the hut.

Obviously, temperance was unheard of. The clergy felt it was their obligation to sip a tipple when visiting a parishioner's home. Physicians prescribed spirits-based tinctures (coloured herbal extracts made with alcohol) and elixirs to cure just about everything from dyspepsia to lumbago. Shopkeepers left a barrel of spirits and a drinking cup for patrons as a complimentary shopping service. Government officials collected taxes from grain suppliers and distillers. Alcohol was accepted as necessary for good health.

YO! HO! HO!

Another spirits category emerged at the turn of the seventeenth century that had a significant impact on the world economy: rum. This spirit created more ignominy than any other, due in part to the influence of Dutch trade in the Caribbean.

Chartered in 1621, the Dutch West India Company had a hand in boosting the exportation of sugar products from Bahia and Pernambuco, especially after the company captured and maintained a good portion of Brazil's northeastern "sugar coast" for over a decade. According to Portuguese registers, during the 1630s, plantations in Pernambuco exported large barrels of cachaça along with lump sugar.

According to some historical sources, in 1637, Dutch émigré Pietr Blower brought sugar cane seedlings and alembics to the British colony on Barbados. Previously settled in Brazil, Blower encouraged the locals to distil molasses as a way to extend the value of each harvest. The British had settled in Barbados 10 years earlier, attempting to establish crops of indigo. Until Blower introduced the sugar cane production and distillation, the island colony's economic fate had been grim. A few years later, a traveller to the island named Henry Colt noted that Barbadians were "devourers upp of hott waters [sic] and such good distillers thereof."

Similarly, a Dutch Jew who emigrated from Brazil, in 1644, named Benjamin Da Costa introduced both sugar mill and distillery equipment to French colonists on the island of Martinique, who had settled there under orders from Cardinal

Richelieu and also suffered from poor financial prospects.

There is scant detail that Spanish colonists on the island of Cuba had also experimented with distilling *aguardiente de caña* by 1598, Cuban historian Miguel Bonera uncovered an early mention of Cuban *aguardiente de caña* distillation, dating from 1643, in which Concillor Alvaro de Luces stated in a meeting that: "in almost all the sugar mills they make *aguardiente de cachaza* and in others *aguardiente de caña ...* which they sell in their bars."

The American colonists loaded their alembics with fermented molasses purchased by the barrel from the Caribbean. The first New England rum distillery was built in Boston in 1657, not long after the Pilgrims arrived on board the *Mayflower*, in 1620 and established the Massachusetts colony. (The Dutch followed in 1664, making "brandy-wine" from molasses in New Amsterdam, which is now known as New York City.)

Author Alice Morse Earle recorded in her 1900 book *Stage Coach and Tavern Days* that:

In 1673 Barbadoes rum was worth 6s. a gallon. In 1687 its price had vastly fallen, and New England rum sold for 1s. 6d. a gallon. In 1692 2s. a gallon was the regular price. In 1711 the price was 3s. 3d. In 1757, as currency grew valueless, it was 21s. a gallon. In 1783 only a little over a shilling; then it was but 8d. a quart. During this time the average cost of molasses in the West Indies was 12d. a gallon; so, though the distillery plant for its production was costly, it can be seen that the profits were great.

Economy will out, it was noted that by 1750, "the quantity of spirits which they distil in Boston from the molasses which they import is as surprising as the cheapness at which they sell it, which is under two shillings a gallon; but they are more famous for the quantity and cheapness than for the excellency of their rum."

Cuba benefited most from the establishment of these northern distilleries. Here were eager consumers of molasses, a commodity that was cheaper to produce than sugar. Shipping the product was cheap because of their proximity to the Caribbean.

Brazil, on the other hand, suffered set back after set back. The local government in Bahia, in 1635, prohibited the sale of cachaça followed by an initial attempt to prohibit the manufacture of cachaça, which led to the burning of some distilleries.

Concurrently, the French, Dutch and British ramped up sugar and rum production on their Caribbean colonies. The price of sugar crashed with increased supply. In addition a combined French and British ban on Brazilian sugar limited its marketability.

Strained relations with Spain between 1640 and 1688 forced the Portuguese crown to depend heavily on Brazil to pay for its military efforts at home. Plantation owners were hit with high taxes on not only sugar, but cachaça. This led to the 1660 Revolt of Cachaça in and around Rio de Janeiro. Once the rebellion was suppressed the next year, the sale of cachaça was banned, leaving producers no recourse but to step up shipment of the spirit to Angola for bartering.

Besides the increase in exportation costs, the price of the slaves rose due to stiffer competition. Somehow, the sugar mills and distilleries of Pernambuco and São Paulo continued to thrive while operations in other regions failed before the ban was lifted in 1695.

Cuban settlers, however, watched with envy as their Jamaican, Barbadan and Martiniquaise neighbours grew fat on the profits from sugar and rum. The Spanish were dazzled by the glittering riches found in their new colonies in Mexico and South America. Cuba was little more than a staging post on the route from the silver mines of Peru to the court of Spain: Havana was little more than a garrison town. The island's ranches, tobacco farms and other agricultural enterprises were thriving, but much of the wealth produced in Cuba flowed directly into Spanish coffers.

If the distillers of western Cuba hoped live in comparable splendour to Jamaican rum producers, they were in for a further disappointment. By the start of the eighteenth century – as rum punch was becoming a populist drink across Europe and the North American colonies – the protectionist Spanish court banned distillation in their territorial possessions to safeguard domestic wine and brandy production.

Cuban *aguardiente de caña* producers ignored the decree, but the extensive exports necessary for growth were out of the question. It wasn't until the British occupied the island for eleven months between 1762 and 1763 that they received some relief. Although the British were masters of Cuba for less than a year, the occupation signalled a change in the island's fortunes. Four thousand slaves were imported during this brief occupation, indicating the British intent to exploit Cuba's potential as a sugar colony.

Indeed, after Britain returned Cuba to Spanish control in exchange for Florida in the Treaty of Paris, the transformation continued. The ban on distilling was lifted. Havana's cane spirits were soon praised "as excellent and sweet as the island's sugar."

THE TRIANGLE TRADE

Why were New World colonies along the American side of the Atlantic making rum? Three reasons: New Englanders could get the molasses from the Caribbean cheaply since it was cheap for the Caribbean colonists to produce it. All of them could distil rum for considerably less than they could import brandy, gin and whisky. Plus, a secondary profit emerged in trading the rum for slaves.

The "triangle trade", aptly nicknamed the "infernal triangle", grew from an incident that occurred over a century earlier when the young Christopher Columbus began his apprenticeship, in 1473, as a business agent for the Genoese Centurione, Di Negro and Spinola trading families. One of the families' most lucrative commodities was sugar. Traveling from the Mediterranean to northern Europe, he learned the trading value of sugar, eventually moving to Madeira and Porto Santo. There, he married Filipa Moniz Perestrello, daughter of Porto Santo's governor Bartolomeu Perestrello, a Portuguese nobleman of Genoese origin.

Madeira was already established as a major sugar-producing centre. Its plantation owners had grown rich from the islands' abundant harvests. Columbus knew from living there for nearly decade there was profit in planting and trading "white gold."

According to Fernando Campoamor, in his landmark 1985 book *El Hijo Alegre de la Caña de Azúcar*, Columbus brought sugar cane seedlings with him, in 1493, on his second voyage to the Caribbean. But there is a sad footnote to this milestone. The great explorer was unable to conduct the cultivation experiments he intended to perform in Hispañola. The delicate plants did not survive the sea crossing.

Pedro di Atienza met with greater success in 1501 when he imported and planted sugar cane seedlings on Hispañola. It was then that the early settlers discovered sugar cane could flourish in the tropical Caribbean climate. Colonists on the island of Puerto Rico copied his efforts in 1506.

Peaceful coexistence amongst the indigenous people of Cuba and the Spanish explorers was fleeting. Columbus's two visits to Cuba never developed into the establishment of a settlement. In fact, his sole quest along the Cuban coast was to find a fabled land of gold he was certain existed nearby – in Japan.

Spanish settlement of Cuba came abruptly and violently in 1512, when conquistadors Diego Velásquez de Cuéllar and his secretary Hernán Cortés arrived with three hundred men and fresh sugar cane seedlings. They forced the Taínos to plant the shoots in the newly bared earth after clearing the lush tropical forest that had been their home. The success of this crop led Cortés to attempt sugar cane cultivation in Mexico a few years later.

By 1515, seven cities were established on Cuba: Santiago de Cuba, Bayamo, Trinidad, Havana, Baracoa, Camagüey and Sancti Spiritus. Velásquez became the island's governor, Cortés the mayor of Santiago de Cuba. Velásquez and Cortés stopped looking for gold in Cuba. Within two decades, the Spanish were certain the legendary El Dorado – the Golden Man – and his city resided in South America, where conquistadors found the palaces, gardens and people of the Inca Empire gilded in gold.

The conquistadors who remained in Cuba turned their attentions to the wealth that could be had in sugar. By 1570, the majority of the 270 Spanish families settled in Cuba had established sprawling sugar plantations and operated sugar mills. Sugar was a labour-intensive proposition. First, land needed to be cleared of lush vegetation for planting. It takes 5,000 to 8,000 seed-cane stems to produce one acre of hand-planted sugar cane. Once it matured (in about eighteen months), the *macheteros* wielded heavy machetes in the sweltering heat to cut the cane as close to the bottom as possible because the lower portion of the stalk is much higher in sucrose.

The intense stench of rotting cane consumed workers in the sugar mills as it was simpler to harvest than to process. According to reports written by missionary Bartolomé de las Casas, colonist Miguel de Ballester and a person named Aguiló discovered that a native tool called a *cunyaya* was effective for extracting cane juice. But even this took great strength and energy to employ. The heat in the sugar mills was so intense that workers were rotated in four-hour cycles to crush the cane, to boil the juice, to skim the hot liquid, to transfer it from kettle to kettle to reduce the developing syrup into crystals, all while maintaining a fire to provide enough heat for the process.

At first the Taínos were forced into labour, housed in squalid conditions. Foreign germs such as smallpox, scarlet fever and tuberculosis killed as many or more labourers than the backbreaking work and physical abuse at the hands of the plantation and sugar mill owners.

One man stood in defence of the native Cubans, Fray Bartolomé de las Casas. The first priest to be ordained in the New World, de las Casas arrived in the Caribbean, in 1502, with his father. He entered the Dominican order eight years later, becoming a missionary, in 1512, to the tormented Taínos. Eyewitness

to the genocide of his spiritual flock by Velàsquez's conquistadors, in 1515, de las Casas penned an impassioned letter begging King Ferdinand to end the devastation. With encouragement from Archbishop Jimenez de Cisneros of Toledo, Ferdinand appointed de las Casas Priest-procurator of the Indies, protector of the Taínos.

But the genocide did not diminish. De las Casas returned to Spain four years later to plead his case once again, this time before King Charles I. His mission met with failure. Unable to gain political support he wrote an inflammatory account of the atrocities in 1523, which became the basis for his 1542 book, *A Brief Account of the Destruction of the Indies: Or, a faithful NARRATIVE OF THE Horrid and Unexampled Massacres, Butcheries and all manner of Cruelties, that Hell and Malice could invent, committed by the Popish Spanish Party on the inhabitants of West-India, TOGETHER With the Devastations of several Kingdoms in America by Fire and Sword, for the space of Forty and Two Years, from the time of its first Discovery by them*, stating that:

> *The Spaniards first assaulted the innocent Sheep, so qualified by the*

Almighty, as is premention'd, like most cruel Tygers, Wolves and Lions hunger-starv'd, studying nothing, for the space of Forty Years, after their first landing, but the Massacre of these Wretches, whom they have so inhumanely and barbarously butcher'd and harass'd with several kinds of Torments, never before known, or heard (of which you shall have some account in the following Discourse) that of Three Millions of Persons, which lived in Hispañola itself, there is at present but the inconsiderable remnant of scarce Three Hundred. Nay the Isle of Cuba, which extends as far, as Valledolid in Spain is distant from Rome, lies now uncultivated, like a Desert and intomb'd in its own Ruins.

De las Casas's pleas and prayers were partially answered in 1537, when Pope Paul III issued Papal Bull *Sublimis Deus* [the Higher God], which declared the indigenous people of the West Indies rational beings with souls and that their lives and property should be protected. Five years later, the Church's stand on the subject compelled King Charles I to sign laws, which prohibited enslavement of the indigenous people. Although the first African slaves were smuggled into the Caribbean in 1514, it wasn't until these laws were set into motion –

coupled with the realization of enormous profits from sugar – that the full-scale slave trade began in the Caribbean.

There is a chain of events that few historians properly report on this subject. The slave trade existed within Africa and the East Indies since the 1100s, primarily instigated by West African kings. Tribesmen from Central and South African territories and kingdoms were captured and sold by Angolan and Ivory Coast chiefs who had an affinity for akpeteshi or burukutu [date-palm wine], which was not dissimilar to the sugar-cane arrack exported by traders from India, Indonesia and Malaysia. Often, those enslaved were unwanted rivals for territory and resources kidnapped or hunted down and shipped to parts unknown.

This societal framework facilitated the development of the international slave trade during the next century as colonists in Brazil and the Caribbean made lucrative deals with these kings. Date-palm wine and similar fermented beverages (not distilled spirits) were integral to West African culture and ritual. Consequently, rum, rhum and cachaça (sold under the name "jeretiba") were quickly recognized as more powerful versions of a favoured commodity. Many economists cite this international exchange of distilled spirits for human cargo as the birth of capitalism and the global economy.

Rum from the Caribbean and New England, and cachaça from Brazil were not the only commodities traded. But in terms of production cost and return on investment, these liquid assets had the highest yield.

The only reason Cuba and Hispaniola did not get involved in this trade of spirits in exchange for slaves at this early stage was because the Spanish government banned the building and operation of distillation equipment in its colonies. The crown wanted to protect its very lucrative brandy and wine export trade. With Mexican colonists making mezcal and other Caribbean colonies making *aguardiente de caña*, it was a tough fight.

What of the association amongst slaves, indentured servants and these new spirits? It became a common practice to provide a daily ration of spirit as compensation, though this has been grossly misinterpreted by generations of historians. Remember: everyone drank at least a half pint of spirit a day to maintain good health, to ward off

the ill effects of water- and food-borne pathogens. It wasn't a matter of keeping slaves drunk and subdued.

Ironically, Brazilian and Caribbean slaves also made their own fermented drinks: cagaça and tafia, respectively. Neither was a distilled spirit. But the name cagaça does lend itself to confusion with the spirit cachaça and likely led to the assumption that the two were the same.

RUM BY ANY OTHER NAME

Speculation surrounds the origins of the word "rum". Some people have said it was derived from the word "rummage". But that term actually dates back to 1582 and implies that a person is making a thorough search of something or some place. Others have said the word was born from the British word "rummer" – or German roemer – which is a type of wine glass. But these vessels appeared in Europe at the same time as the cane-juice liquor. One romantic suggestion holds that "rum" is an abbreviated version of "rumney", a type of wine made in Greece and the southern Balkans similar to the sweet dessert wine called mavrodaphne.

According to nineteenth-century philologist Walter William Skeat, the term is an Anglicised version of the

Malay word "*brum*," which is an arrack made from sugar cane juice. Historian Frederick H. Smith found that the first documented use of the word "rum" appears in a plantation deed recorded in Barbados in 1650, which identifies the Three Houses estate in St. Philip parish as having "four large mastick cisterns for liquor for Rum."

A year later, Barbardos resident Giles Silvester made the only known reference linking the words "rum" and "rumbullion" when he wrote: "the chiefe fudling they make in the Iland is Rumbullions, als Kill Divill, and this is made of Suggar cones distilled in a hott hellish and terrible liquor." The term "rumbullion" was a common word in Devonshire, England that means "a great tumult."

However its birth came about, the word "rum" was adopted throughout the Caribbean in the seventeenth century. First appearing in the 1750s in Diderot and Alembert's *Encyclopedie*, the word "*rhum*" with an "h" is specifically used to describe rums made in French colonies such as Martinique and Guadeloupe. The word "*ron*," indicates the sugar cane liquor was produced in Spanish colonies, the most famous of which is the island of Cuba.

RUM RATIONS BY LAND AND BY SEA

Unlike the other new world spirits, rum received naval support. The British Royal Navy practically required alcohol consumption within its ranks. However, the one-gallon daily beer ration was not exactly an incentive for sailors to join the navy. Nathaniel Knott, in his 1634 book, *Advice of a Seaman*, wrote a humorous account of the poor quality of navy beer saying that:

> The brewers have gotten the art to sophisticate beer with broom instead of hops, and ashes instead of malt, and (to make it more lively) to pickle it with salt water so that, whilst it is new, it shall seemingly be worthy of praise, but in one month wax worse than stinking water.

Apparently, beer quality did not improve over time. In his 1761 "appeal to the public to prevent the Navy being supplied with pernicious provisions," William Thompson, stated that the rationed beer "stands as abominably as the foul stagnant water which is pumped out of many cellars in London at the midnight hour and the sailors were under the necessity of shutting their eyes and stopping their breath by holding their noses before they could conquer their aversion so as to prevail upon themselves in their extreme necessities to drink it."

Admiral Robert Blake, in 1650, substituted brandy for his sailors' beer ration. However, his decision had nothing to do with the wretched quality of the beer. Space on navy ships was a valuable commodity and brandy took up far less cargo space.

In 1655, Vice-Admiral William Penn (later to become the founder of Pennsylvania) arrived in Barbados and captured Jamaica during his campaign to claim the West Indies on behalf of Britain's head of state Oliver Cromwell. During the long ocean voyage, the daily beer and wine rations ran out and the French brandy given to officers was frowned upon: a casualty from the Thirty Years War, when French and German products were generally banned in Britain.

Rum was plentiful. Rum was cheap. Rum was familiar to the sailors who had encountered cachaça since Elizabethan times. It gave Penn the perfect reason to initiate the rum ration amongst the fleet sailing the Caribbean. Other fleets adopted the same practice. By 1687 rum was decreed an official part of sailors' daily rations. In 1731, the gallon of beer ration was completely replaced with a half pint of 140–170 proof rum (equivalent to a pint of 80 proof) in "Regulations and Instructions Relating to His Majesty's Service at Sea." It was a practice that continued until the 1970s.

Proof. The word "proof" originated from a simple test to measure the alcohol content in spirits by pouring the liquor onto gunpowder and igniting it. If the powder burned, it indicated that there was sufficient alcohol – or proof. This was deemed 100 proof, though it is actually around 57 percent ABV. This test replaced less accurate measures such as igniting a piece of cloth soaked in spirit to see if the spirit would burn cleanly away without harming the cloth or simply attempting to ignite the spirit.

The navy didn't always have to pay for its rum. Ships were frequently given free or deeply discounted casks of rum by Caribbean sugar planters to encourage the fleet's frequent returns to port. The practice ensured an island's safety from marauding pirates, who also fancied rum.

Another spirit accompanied the fleets. British Royal Navy officers drank gin, easily procured in the navy's home port of Plymouth in Devonshire, where there were plenty of malting houses and gin distilleries.

Because of its cheap price, rum – or whiskey – rationing became common practice on land as well, amongst farmers and shopkeepers who issued farm hands and apprentices a ration of spirits twice daily. It was a most generous work incentive. For example, in 1738, it was recorded in Northampton, Massachusetts, that 10 gallons of rum were ordered to serve to the men building the new meeting house. In Northfield, Massachusetts, circa 1763, two barrels of New England rum and four gallons of Jamaica rum were doled out during the construction of its new meeting house.

Throughout the northern United States, it was also common practice for workers to be paid in liquor rather than coin or paper in addition to the liquor they drank on the job. In the south, workers might find themselves paid in drink or tobacco.

But spirits weren't just a work incentive. According to a 1920 article about life in early Puritan New England, "bars were actually set up at the church door, and free rum and other heady 'lick-quers' given to everybody." As

recently as 1825 worshippers at the First Congregationalist Church of New Haven, Connecticut, were treated to an adjacent free bar.

Rum could also be considered to be Australia's first currency. Workers erecting the first church in Sydney were partly paid in rum. Sydney's first hospital was called the Rum Hospital since it was financed by local businessmen in 1810 in return for a contract that licensed them to import 60,000 gallons of rum to sell to colonists. (In the eyes of in-coming governor Lachlan Macquarie, it was the only way he could ensure the colony had medical facilities that progressed beyond the tents and temporary buildings used for the purpose since its establishment in 1788.) The reward for the capture of Australia's first bush ranger was set at five gallons of rum. And it was said that a wife could be purchased for four gallons of the spirit.

GLUGGING GROG & THE BIRTH OF THE DAIQUIRÍ

The world was drinking. The world was drinking a lot. One person did express some concern over the amount that was consumed in those days. The British Royal Navy's Vice-Admiral Edward Vernon (nicknamed Old Grog because of the waterproof grogam made from gum-stiffened silk, wool and mohair that he wore on deck) issued an order on 21 August 1740 that the daily rum ration should be: "…every day mixed with the proportion of a quart of water to a half pint of rum, to be mixed in a scuttled butt kept for that purpose, and to be done upon the deck, and in the presence of the Lieutenant of the Watch who is to take particular care to see that the men are not defrauded in having their full allowance of rum…and let those that are good husband men receive extra lime juice and sugar that to be made more palatable to them."

The men were issued two servings of this potion per day: There was a call to "up spirits" between 10 am and noon and another from 4 pm to 6 pm.

Grog
1 part rum
4 parts water
Optional: sugar and lime to taste
Build in a tumbler and serve.

The word "groggy" entered the language at this time: first, to describe the effect Grog had on sailors, especially those with low alcohol tolerance and second to describe those who saved their morning rations to combine with their evening rations. But it seems the Royal Navy was one of the last to adopt a rum drink that had spread rapidly across the Caribbean.

This Grog – a rum, sugar, lime juice and water concoction – had another name, Punch. British East India Company seamen, freebooters and adventurers travelling the Indian Ocean in the early 1600s quickly adopted Punch (derived from *panch*, the Hindi term for the number "five"). Made from five ingredients: sugar, lemon, water, tea and arrack, this libation lured the sipper with the exotic tastes of citrus, sugar and tea that were otherwise unknown in seventeenth-century Europe. It is likely that the citrus juice coupled with the addictive sweetness of sugar made this drink irresistible to scurvy-prone, vitamin-C-deficient sailors.

Punch
1 part arrack or rum
4 parts brewed tea
lime juice to taste
sugar to taste
Build in a tumbler and serve.

In the West Indies, one would be pretty hard pressed to find a local source for tea. Already popular at home, it was no surprise that seamen crafted a rum version. Captain William Dampier mentioned how widespread this Punch was in his 1699 memoirs, *A New Voyage Round the World*, commenting that while he was on the island of Tortuga he noticed:

> *Ships coming from some of the Caribbean islands are always well stored with Rum, Sugar and Lime-juice to make Punch, to hearten their Men when they are at work getting and bringing aboard the Salt; and they commonly provide the more, in hopes to meet with Privateers, who resort hither in the aforesaid Months, purposely to keep a Christmas, as they call it, being sure to meet with Liquor enough to be merry with, and are very liberal to those that treat them.*

This British drink was known as Ponche by the Spanish, defined in the 1769 edition of *Nouveau Dictionnaire de Sobrino, François, Espanol et Latin* as: "*bebida Inglesa, que le hace aguardiente, agua, limon y azucar* [an English drink made with rum, water, lime and sugar]."

Reaching the French Caribbean, this drink became known as Ti Punch, a contraction of *Petit* [little] *Punch*. As these ingredients are identical to those in the Daiquirí, it becomes clear that the Daiquirí was not so much invented as named in the late 1800s.

Grog and Punch were not much different from another invention we mentioned earlier, the Mojito's predecessor, El Draque. Neither were they far removed from the Toddy (potentially another Hindi loanword found in documented accounts about the British experience in India circa 1671), which combined hot water and lemon juice with rum plus a dose of the ever-present nutmeg garnish. British pirates who roamed the Caribbean had yet another potation if the citrus stores ran out called Bumboo: rum blended with sugar, water and a grating of nutmeg.

Bumboo
1 part rum
4 parts water
Sugar to taste
Build in a tumbler and serve topped
*   with fresh grated nutmeg.*

Toddy
1 part rum
4 parts water
lemon juice to taste
Build in a tumbler and serve with a
*   grating of nutmeg.*

Back to Grog and Punch or Ponche. These three drinks arrived in Havana when the city was captured by the British on 6 June 1762, when at dawn, a British fleet, comprising more than 50 ships and a combined force of over 11,000 men of the Royal Navy and Army, sailed into Cuban waters and made an amphibious landing east of what was then the third largest city in the New World.

The Daiquirí's other parent, the Canchanchara, appeared throughout the island a few decades later, mixing rum, lime juice and honey. Were Cubans influenced by the navy's Grog, the pirate's Bumboo and the regular seaman's Punch to divine a quencher to refresh workers in the sugar cane fields? We think it is very possible.

GETTING PUNCHY

Blogger ian Lender posted an interesting item, in December of 2008, that exemplifies the staggeringly close relationship between Punch and the British Royal Navy. It appears that in 1694, British Lord Admiral Edward Russell hosted an officer's party in which the *piece de resistance* was a Punch containing 250 gallons of brandy, 125 gallons of Malaga wine, 1,400 pounds of sugar, 2,500 lemons, 20 gallons of lime juice and 5 pounds of nutmeg that was blended in the establishment's garden fountain.

(A popular spice amongst travellers and seagoing folk, nutmeg improved the taste of just about anything, especially poorly stored meats, pasty pastry and table wine. It wasn't cheap. Thus, it became an early form of bling. In Britain, a nutmeg cost more than an ounce of gold and was a prized possession from the sixteenth through the eighteenth centuries. Londoners were occasionally known to flaunt their wealth by wearing a nutmeg grater around their necks – or to at least carry one with them – and add their personal nutmeg garnish to dishes and drinks in restaurants.)

The servers at Admiral Russell's party worked in 15-minute shifts, paddling around in a small wooden canoe and filling guests' cups. The shifts were short in order to avoid the danger of being overcome by alcohol fumes, falling overboard and drowning. It did rain during this gregarious event but it did not stop revellers from partaking of the immense flowing bowl.

A silk canopy was erected over the fountain to prevent dilution of its contents. Why such a long party? It took a week to finish the contents of this immense punch bowl.

Not everyone used such a gregarious

container for serving this delightful drink. But many people did assign a certain amount of panache when "the Monteith" came into fashion around 1697:

The rim was scalloped like its namesake's coat, or cut in battlements, thus forming indentations, in which a punch ladle and lemon strainer and tall wine-glasses were hung on their sides, the foot out. The rim was usually separate from the bowl, and was lifted off with the glasses and ladle and strainer, for the punch to be brewed in the bowl. When the punch was duly finished, the ornamental rim was replaced.

The Monteith is said to have been invented to chill glassware, the scalloped rim set in place to hold the stems before it came into common use as a punchbowl. Who was Montieth? We may never know, as there is little written about him, except this couplet quoted in William King's 1708 *The Art of Cookery*:

New things produce new words and thus Monteith, Has by one vessel saved his name from death.

The early 1700s opened with the Whigs adopting punch as their unofficial party drink, quickly followed by the Tories who couldn't resist the "flowing bowl" either.

Punch was an infinitely variable tipple by custom. It gave both mixer and imbiber an endless variety of options: with tea, without tea, change the nutmeg for mace, switch lemon for lime, rum or brandy or wine or port instead of arrack. There was only one golden rule: make it festive. Consequently, nobles, merchants, shopkeepers and just about everyone in between could afford to share a few cups of some form of Punch.

Tavern keepers kept up with the times, adding Punch, Grog and Toddy to their bills of fare. Punches became proprietary creations. Fraunces Tavern in New York City became famous for the bowls that proprietor and freed slave Samuel Fraunces turned out. The site of Washington's farewell address to the Continental Army in 1783, Fraunces Tavern was also rented out to house the offices of the United States Departments of War, the Treasury and Foreign Affairs when New York City became the nation's first capitol. Thus, Samuel Fraunces was the first caterer to the US Congress and the President. (The tavern is still in operation today.)

At the time, spirituous libations often were served in small tumblers. The blending of sugar, water and juice into glass only required a wooden or metal toddy-stick for stirring:

The toddy stick, beloved for the welcome ringing music it made on the sides of glass tumblers, was used to stir up toddy and other sweetened drinks.

It was a stick six or eight inches long, with a knob at one end, or flattened out at the end so it would readily crush the loaf sugar used in the drink. The egg-nog stick was split at one end, and a cross-piece of wood was set firmly in. It was a crude egg-beater. Whirled rapidly around, while the upright stick was held firmly between the palms of the hands, it was a grateful, graceful and inviting machine in the hands of skilful landlords of old.

Author Kingsley Amis commented in his 1972 book *On Drink* that: "Not only is drink here to stay; the moral seems to be that when it goes, we go too." It should be pretty obvious by now that during the eighteenth century, alcohol was an essential part of life and that by the late 1700s mixed drinks had come into the mainstream both on land and on the sea.

Standing upright and ganging up to eat, keeping warm, reproducing and laughing were all accompanied by spirits. Political machines were fuelled by them. Civilisation knew the pleasures of alcohol and as a whole was poised for a drinking revolution.

C H A P T E R   S I X
All the Day & All of the Night

A DRINK EXPLOSION & THE REVOLUTIONARY SPIRIT

We keep reminding you that early in history, water could be a most dangerous liquid to consume without alcohol. So much so that by the 1700s, there wasn't a moment gone by that you wouldn't sip a tipple of some form or another. Whether you lived in Europe or in the colonies, the average person had a pretty impressive menu of libations to consume each and every day.

An eye-opener of brandy or rum started the day (possibly a carry-over over from the Scottish Highlanders' traditional morning dram of whisky). Breakfast included a bit of rum with bacon or bread soaked in beer. (Small beer, a sometimes unfiltered low-alcohol beer sometimes as thick as porridge was also popular. Though its alcohol level of around two percent was too low to destroy water-borne pathogens, yeast also excretes carbon and acids that render its environment less hospitable to competing bacteria.) By 11 am, everyone stopped work for an "eleven o'clock bitters". Around noontime, dinner was served at the local tavern offered up with one of many popular "small drinks," many of them recognizable as British and French mixed drinks: Bumboo, Calibogus, Cherry Bounce, Ebulum, Manathan, Meridian, Mimbo, Rattle-skull, Rum Flip, Sangaree, Stonewall, Switchel, Syllabub, Whistle-belly Vengeance, Yard of Flannel.

Calibogus
Build equal parts beer and aged rum in a tumbler. Stir and serve.

Cherry Bounce
25 oz [750 ml] dark rum
5 pints [2.5 litres] cherries, washed and de-stemmed.
Crush cherries with pits in. Place crushed cherries into a clean wide-mouth bottle or jar. Add rum. Let it sit for a week. Strain. Add demerara sugar to taste. Let sit one more week.

Ebulum
Infuse elderberry juice with juniper berries. Add cardamom pods and

cinnamon sticks for spice. Let it sit for a week. Strain. Sweeten to taste with demerara sugar. let sit for one more week.

Manathan
Build 1 part rum with 4 parts beer in a tumbler. Add sugar to taste.

Meridian
Build 1 part brandy with 4 parts strong tea in a tumbler.

Mimbo
Build 1 part rum to 3 parts water in a tumbler. Add sugar to taste.

Rattle-skull
Build 1 part brandy, 1 part rum, 1 part wine and 3 parts porter in a tumbler. Garnish with a grating of nutmeg and a thin slice of lime peel.

Rum Flip
This popular New England potion, dating as far back as 1690, was made by filling a 64 oz [2 litre] pitcher with 48 oz [140 cl] beer. Add 8 oz [240 ml] aged rum. Sweeten to taste with molasses or muscovado sugar or dried pumpkin. Stir with a red-hot poker.

"Taverns which pretended to great gentility and elegance kept on hand a bowl of flip-sweetener made of a pint of cream, four pounds of sugar and four eggs, well beaten together."

Sangaree
The British spin-off of a Spanish sangria, a simple sangaree mixes 1 wine-glass [8 oz / 240 ml] Madeira and 0.5 oz [15 ml] hot water with 1 lump of sugar in a tumbler. Stir and garnish with a grating of nutmeg.

Stonewall
Build equal parts rum and hard cider in a tumbler.

Switchel
A favourite in Salem, Massachusetts during the 1600s, Dr Benjamin Rush wrote a pamphlet that recommended "its use by harvest laborers." Build 4 oz [120 ml] apple cider vinegar, 2 oz [60 ml] molasses, 4 oz [120 ml] honey, 2 tsp ground ginger in a pitcher with water to make 2 quarts [1.9 litres]. Stir to dissolve everything. Serve in a tumbler with a dash of dark aged rum.

Syllabub
Build equal parts heavy cream whisked until stiff and Madeira or Marsala. Add sugar and grated nutmeg to taste.

Whistle-belly Vengeance
"It was sour household beer simmered in a kettle, sweetened with molasses, filled with crumbs of "ryneinjun" bread, and drunk

piping hot; its name was whistle-belly-vengeance, or whip-belly-vengeance. This name was not a Yankee vulgarism, but a well-known old English term. Bickerdyke says small beer was rightly stigmatized by this name.'"

Yard of Flannel

Beat 4 eggs, 4 oz [120 ml] aged rum, 3 oz [90 ml] sugar, 0.5 tsp ground cinnamon, 0.5 tsp ground nutmeg in a bowl until light and foamy. Heat 1 quart [960 ml] hard apple cider to just under a boil. Slowly pour the cider into the egg mixture, whisking constantly to avoid curdling. Whisk until creamy. Serve in punch cups.

Four o'clock tea was a repeat of the "eleven o'clock bitter." Supper included a beer, hard cider, perry or spirits. And then it was off to the tavern at 8 pm for a pint or two, followed by a nightcap of hotchpotch (a Manathan served warm) to cut the chill and damp before bedtime.

Prices for these concoctions were sometimes regulated by the local court as in the case of Salem, New Jersey, where in 1729, taverns' prices were dictated as follows:

A rub of punch made with double-refined sugar and one and a half gills of rum .... 9d.

A rub of punch made with single refined sugar and one and a half gills of rum ....8d.

A rub made of Muscovado sugar and one and a half gills of rum .... 7d.

A quart of flipp made with a pint of rum .... 9d.

A pint of wine .... 1s.

A gill of rum .... 3d.

A quart of strong beer .... 4d.

A gill of brandy or cordial .... 6d.

A quart of metheglin .... 9d.

A quart of cider royal .... 8d.

A quart of cider .... 4d.

Taverns were the social core on both sides of the Atlantic. Men met to discuss the latest crops, to auction livestock, to tell tales of adventures and to hold meetings of the Freemasons. The first lodge in America, St John's Lodge gathered, in 1733, at the Bunch of Grapes in Boston.

The tavern was the place to get the local news and gossip. Beginning in the 1730s, it was also the place to discourse about the politics of two nations that collided over the production of spirits.

TAXATION WITHOUT REPRESENTATION

The sugar and molasses act of 1733 passed by the British Parliament on 17 May, under the reign of King George II (1683–1760), was proposed by sugar planters in the British West Indies, who wanted the government's help to force the rum-producing American colonies to buy their goods, not the cheaper sugar and molasses offered by Brazil plus the Spanish and French Caribbean islands, The law stated that:

> from and after… [December 25, 1733]…there shall be raised, levied, collected and paid, unto and for the use of his Majesty…, upon all rum or spirits of the produce or manufacture of any of the colonies or plantations in America, not in the possession or under the dominion of his Majesty…

The tax was high. Nine pence was levied on every gallon of non-British rum, molasses or syrup imported to British colonies. Six pence was charged on every gallon of foreign sugar. This didn't really affect homeland British businesses. It could have caused hardship for American distilleries, if the distillers had not started smuggling molasses and bribing harbour officials. In truth, British enforcement officers were blissfully unaware of what was happening in the colonies.

At the time, the British government took a tacit stance of "salutary neglect" with regard to trade in North America. The big money was being made in Caribbean sugar as well as in Asian and African coffee, tea and spices.

Then the French and Indian War (1754–1763) tapped the British government's resources to the quick. Britain gained all of North America east of the Mississippi coupled with a promise from France that it would not try to colonize the Crown's even more valuable holdings in India. Spain received New Orleans and lands west of Mississippi as payment for their aid to the British side.

But Britain still had to pay dearly for the employment of its Royal Navy, the army and for help from the Dutch Republic, Sweden and Portugal. King George III was enthroned, in 1760, to lead a cash-poor government. Not the strongest of monarchs, he suffered from the hereditary blood disease porphyria, which causes bouts of mania and finally chronic mental illness.

Prime Minister George Grenville (1712–1770) had a simple solution to the country's financial crunch. With Parliament's blessing, Grenville instigated the Sugar Act of 1764, which included:

> *For every ton of wine of the growth of the Madeiras, or of any other island or place from whence such wine may be lawfully imported, and which shall be so imported from such islands or places, the sum of seven pounds.*

> *For every ton of Portugal, Spanish, or any other wine (except French wine) imported from Great Britain, the sum of ten shillings.*

> *VI. And be it further enacted by the authority aforesaid, That in lieu and instead of the rate and duty imposed by the said act upon melasses and syrups, there shall…be raised, levied, collected and paid…for and upon every gallon of melasses or syrups, being the growth, product, or manufacture, of any colony or plantation in America, not under the dominion of his Majesty…which shall be imported or brought into any colony or plantation in America, the sum of three pence….*

In short, Grenville was determined to repair Britain's fiscal nightmare by having its colonies cover the bills. And money was one commodity that was plentiful in the New World. But if you read closely, you will notice that Grenville actually proposed a significant tax reduction. Why were the colonists up in arms? Along with the tax break came the threat that the government would stem the tide of "salutary neglect" and compel the colonists to actually pay the tax. In other words, they were going to reduce a tax no one paid, but they finally were going to enforce it. American exports had to be bonded and the New England export trade in lumber and iron plus imports of molasses slacked, creating an economic depression. Not willing to deal with diminished income, tavern patrons led the cry that "taxation without representation is tyranny."

Insult was added to injury. Britain attempted to clear its prisons by sending convicted felons to the colonies as indentured servants. The colonists turned away the ships. Then Grenville slapped the colonies with the Duties in American Colonies Act of 1765 (aka: the Stamp Act) to defray the cost of maintaining a colonial military presence, primarily intended to protect the fur trade, not the settlers.

The act required all legal documents, permits, commercial contracts, newspapers, pamphlets and playing cards printed in the American colonies to carry a tax stamp. On top of that, to be admitted to the bar or to act as a notary, one had to pay a £10 tax (only £2 in Britain).

Regular meetings took place over drinks at Boston's Green Dragon Tavern attended by people such as Paul Revere. Boston tax collector Andrew Oliver found himself burned in effigy soon after. He resigned. (His predecessor Samuel Adams, son of the Boston brewer and familiar face in the city's taverns, had used non-collection of nearly £1,000 in taxes as a political bargaining chip before positioning himself as the leader of many town meetings and drafter of many protests against the Stamp Act.)

Three hundred fifty members of the Sons of Liberty, revolutionaries who were extremely upset with the existing government, drank and dined on three barbecued pigs in a tent at the Liberty Tree Tavern in Dorchester, Massachusetts. They raised 45 toasts to everything from revolutionaries around the world to the speedy removal of their taskmasters. However, John Adams wrote of the night in his diary, that he "did not see one person intoxicated."

Fraunces Tavern in New York, the Sabin Tavern in Providence and the Black Horse Inn in Winchester, Massachusetts, were just a few of the establishments where the Sons of Liberty met over drinks to determine the best means of retaliation. The Indian King Tavern and City Tavern in Philadelphia became the gathering spots for Benjamin Franklin's "Junto" of colonial intellectuals and revolutionaries. The Virginia Committee of Correspondence met at the Sir Walter Raleigh Tavern in Williamsburg.

Of course, one problem was inherent with conducting business over so many drinks. Of Boston's Green Dragon Tavern, Revere wrote:

In the fall of 1774 and winter of 1775, I was one of upwards of thirty men, chiefly mechanics, who formed ourselves with a Committee for the purpose of watching the movements of the British soldiers and gaining every intelligence of the movements of the Tories. We held our meetings at the Green Dragon Tavern. This committee were astonished to find all their secrets known to General Gage, although every time they met every member swore not to reveal their transactions even to Hancock, Adams, Otis, Warren or Church.

A REVELLING EFFECT

According to historian Charles Taussig in his 1928 book, *Rum, Romance, and Rebellion*, Paul Revere's famed midnight ride took a spirituous detour before the revolutionary road into history, commenting that: "It appears that Paul Revere was dispatched on his now famous ride not to "spread the alarm, Through every Middlesex village and farm, For the country folk to be up and to arm," but to warn [John] Hancock and [Samuel] Adam to flee and escape arrest and also to tell the patriots of those towns to hide their military stores."

Paul Revere's own narrative of his role on that epochal night claimed that he had not ridden far when he encountered two British horsemen, one of whom closely pursued him until the redcoat rode into a clay pit. Then Revere, "hot under the collar," directly rode to the home of Isaac Hall, Captain of the Medford Minute Men, who owned a rum distillery.

His short stay was long enough for Captain Hall to pour for Revere several "stirrup cups" [a parting cup offered to guests already in the saddle, to entice them back for another round or at least warm their journey forward] of old Medford rum which "would have made a rabbit bite a bulldog."

Revere's resolve and courage was fortified to such a point that "he who came a silent horseman, departed a virile and vociferous crusader, with a cry of defiance and not of fear." Naturally, he was detained by local authorities for an hour before being allowed to continue his ride into the history books.

Alcohol was part of the political fabric of the colonies in other ways as well: buying votes, buying loyalty, celebrating election results. When George Washington campaigned in 1758 for the Virginia House of Burgess, he did it by ladling out a barrel of Barbados rum to prospective voters. Though he won the election, he later complained that his campaign manager had not spent enough money on alcohol.

Barbados rum in particular was a favourite of the first United States President. When he was nineteen years old, he had accompanied his half-brother, in 1751, to the island (the only foreign country he ever visited). His half-brother suffered from tuberculosis and his doctors hoped the tropical warmth would aid in his recovery. While there, young Washington discovered rum. He also went to the theatre for the first time, visited the largest city he had ever seen and saw his first fireworks display.

During the American Revolution, Washington wrote to a congressional leader, in 1777, that: "The benefits of moderate use of liquor have been experienced in all armies and are not to be disputed."

Washington instructed the commissary general of purchases for the Continental Army in that same year that:

There should always be a sufficient quantity of spirits with the army, to furnish moderate supplies to the troops ... such as when they are marching in hot or cold weather, in camp in wet, on fatigue or in working parties, it is so essential that it is not to be dispensed with.

History shows which side won the war. However, alcohol could not be credited entirely for the victory. American troops were defeated at the Battle of Bunker Hill on 17 June 1775, not because they ran out of gunpowder or were in need of reinforcements, as was later written by temperate historians. They lost on that hot summer day because the troops were out of water. The order was given for the rum kegs to be tapped. Then the British soldiers arrived.

In a letter to his mother, militiaman Peter Brown described the fighting:

The danger we were in made us think there was treachery, and that we were brot there to be all slain, and I must and will venture to say that there was treachery, oversight or presumption in the conduct of our officers. And about half after 5 in the morn, we not having above half the fort done, they began to fire, I suppose as soon as they had orders, pretty briskly a few minutes and then stopt and then again to the number of about 20 or more. They killed one of us, and then they ceased till about 11 o'clock and then they began pretty brisk again; and that caused some of our young country people to desert, apprehending the danger in a clearer manner than the rest, who were more diligent in digging and fortifying ourselves against them. We began to be almost beat out, being tired by our labour and having no sleep the night before, but little victuals, no drink but rum...

Although they were defeated by the British (who ended up with a thousand casualties) the Americans, led by General Howe, proved they could make a stand and stemmed the progress of the Siege of Boston.

Even after independence was won, Washington stuck to his spirits. He used rye whiskey and Jamaica rum in his Eggnog. His wife Martha was famed for her Rum Punch. For his inauguration in 1785, as the first United States President, he insisted on having two barrels of Barbados rum on hand to toast the occasion.

Martha Washington's Rum Punch
*4 oz [120 ml] fresh-squeezed orange
    juice
4 oz [120 ml] fresh-squeezed lemon
    juice
4 oz [120 ml] simple syrup
1 orange cut into quarters
3 lemons cut into quarters
1/2 tsp grated nutmeg
3 cinnamon sticks, broken
6 whole cloves
12 oz [360 ml] boiling water*
Combine the orange, lemons, nutmeg, cinnamon sticks and cloves. Muddle the mixture lightly. Add syrup, lemon and orange juice. Pour boiling water over the mixture. Let it cool. Strain out the solids. Stirring constantly, bring the mixture to a boil. Then reduce the heat and simmer for 10 minutes. Refrigerate overnight.

In a punch bowl combine:
*3 parts refrigerated fruit and
    spice mixture*

*1 part light rum
1 part dark rum
1/2 part orange curaçao*
Serve the punch over ice.
Garnish with grated nutmeg
    and cinnamon.

Washington had another favourite spirit that is uniquely American: applejack. He was introduced to this fruit brandy around 1760 by the Laird family of Scobeyville, New Jersey, who had been producing it since 1698. The technique was simple: Hard cider was "jacked" or freeze-distilled. So enamoured with the result, Washington requested and received the recipe, which he then introduced in the Virginia colony.

That same year, another mixed drink of sorts was added to the tavern menu: the sling. Dr Benjamin Rush, a signer of the Declaration of Independence warned Americans against it. Though his views would help to shape the temperance movement and American Prohibition, his "Taste not, handle not" speeches and writings had little impact on consumption during his lifetime.

Rum Sling
*1 part dark rum
1 part water*
Build in a tumbler, stir and serve.

THE SPIRIT OF REBELLION

Although the American Revolution was sparked by British taxes on spirits production, it did not take long for Washington to succumb to the economically lucrative temptation of alcohol taxation. In 1791, he imposed the Whiskey Tax to pay for the construction of the nation's Capitol building. Co-revolutionary Thomas Jefferson resigned his post as Secretary of State in opposition to what he perceived as "big government tactics."

No one in western Pennsylvania approved of this imposition on the right to make a living from the bountiful grain harvests and the distillate they made from the yield. To express their opinion, resistance fighters organised tar-and-feathering expeditions against tax collectors. Washington responded by instigating the Militia Law of 1792, ordering federal marshals to make tax resisters in Pennsylvania, Virginia, West Virginia and North and South Carolina appear in court. It did not work. These rough and hardy immigrants from Scotland and Ireland didn't take such hard-ball tactics sitting down.

This was especially true of the Presbyterian Ulster-Scots (aka: Scots-Irish) who had already had their fill of religious oppression in Scotland and then Northern Ireland, coupled with racial oppression in New England and Canada. The social pressures forced them to migrate to Pennsylvania's Shenandoah Valley, North Carolina's Blue Ridge and Louisiana's swamps.

They supplied the Revolutionary army with their daily half-pint ration of whiskey when New England's rum distillers could not supply troops at great distances. And just like rum before the revolution, whiskey was cheap to produce. The Scots-Irish lived in the wilderness where soil produced abundant grain, hardwood trees were everywhere, fresh water filtered through limestone and waterways for shipping were plentiful.

The 1794 Whiskey Rebellion (aka: Whiskey Insurrection) escalated when 13,000 militia – a force as large as the entire Revolutionary army – marched on the anti-tax distillers living "out west" in Pennsylvania's Allegheny Valley in what is now Monongehela. After a few pitched battles, the rebels hid in the woods or fled the area. Twenty men were captured and paraded down Philadelphia's Market Street. The men were imprisoned. One died. Two were convicted of treason and sentenced to death by hanging. President Washington, however, pardoned both of them on the grounds that one was a "simpleton," and the other was "insane."

Ironically, George Washington himself became a whiskey distiller, in 1797, when his Scottish farm manager James Anderson convinced him that whiskey production was the perfect complement to his grain-milling business. He was right. It soon became Washington's most profitable venture. Lucky for him, the Whiskey Tax was repealed in 1802 by his successor President Thomas Jefferson.

Some distillers such as Daniel Shawhan who produced Monongehela Red Whiskey on his Allegheny County farm moved even before the Whiskey Tax was enacted, to the frontier territories of Kentucky and Tennessee where corn grew far more abundantly than wheat. In 1788, Shawhan and his family set up their farm and distillery in Bourbon County. Elijah Pepper, grandfather to Colonel James E Pepper, settled near Lexington, Kentucky in 1776 and built a log cabin distillery four years later. Jacob Beam set up his still in the same area that same year. Interestingly, most historians credit Reverend Elijah Craig

with making the first bourbon whiskey. But Reverend Craig first made his whiskey, in 1789, at Fort Harrod in Kentucky's Mercer County – not Bourbon County.

Bourbon whiskey. The name is derived from the choice in 1780 to name the units of the Virginia colony that became part of Kentucky after French General Lafayette, who was descended from the French royal House of Bourbon. Thus, in 1785, Bourbon County was founded.

There were hundreds of homestead farmer-distillers already making whiskey in the area, since rum shipments were scarce and expensive, while corn and rye were plentiful. Kentuckians shipped whiskey to New Orleans via the Ohio River connection to the Mississippi. Kentucky became a state, in 1792, though not heavily regulated by the new federal government: it was too far away. That year Bourbon County was cut up into smaller areas including Mason County. But the whiskey produced within the original county boundaries continued to be called "Old Bourbon Whiskey" to remind people of its heritage, not because of its ageing. It even bore that label on casks shipped up and down the river.

Similarly, the settlers who moved to the Tennessee frontier discovered the land offered them a bounty of what they needed to produce whiskey: good soil for growing corn, rye and barley; abundant firewood and white oak for barrels; and a network of rivers for transporting their goods to the more populated colonies. The first recorded distillery in the area was Evan Shelby's East Tennessee distillery in Sapling Grove, established in 1771, which made rye whiskey. More distilleries sprouted up while the government was only taxing them 2s, 6d per gallon.

Business boomed. It boomed to the point that the few officials who governed the area were concerned that all the grain was going to whiskey production. In Davidson County, an act was past by the court, in 1784, that there should be no distilling of alcohol due to a grain shortage. It didn't last. Farmers were doing it. Distillers were doing it. They were making a reported six million gallons a year of it. And all of them were selling it cheap: for about a dollar a gallon.

There was a reason whiskey was in high demand among frontiersmen. It was more than just a drink. It was an antiseptic, an anaesthetic, a disinfectant, a stimulant and a sedative. Very all-purpose stuff.

Not wanting to miss out on the profits, middle Tennesseans also capitalised on the distilling business. In 1787, John "King" Boyd established his distillery-tavern, the Red Heifer, in Nashville. Frederick Stump followed suit, although he had a little setback when a local tribe burned down his business in October 1792. He was up and running three years later and producing 600 gallons a year on four stills.

THE HAIR OF THE DOG

Bitters, vermouth, soda water and absinthe. All four creations appeared during the 1700s, taking their place in the drinks vernacular before the century was out.

In London, provincial clergyman Richard Stoughton received a Royal Patent in 1712 for his alcohol-based infusion of herbs, which he called Stoughton's Elixir. The public dubbed it Stoughton's Bitters. It was the second compound medicine in the world to be issued a patent for its invention. And this digestive bitters gained rapid popularity. Stoughton first imported his concoction to the American colonies in 1730, where it was an overnight sensation.

During the American Revolution, Stoughton's bitters were hard to come by. But this did not stop the demand. By the 1790s, dozens of domestically-produced bitters entered the marketplace. Not all the patent medicines that sprung up after Stoughton's success were digestive or aromatic bitters. A goodly number were the inventions of quacks who wanted to get in on the lucrative action in what would soon be called the "snake oil" trade. The numbers of what we now consider to be bitters, however, increased over tenfold by the early 1800s.

Although the actual recipe died with its inventor, an attempt to replicate it was made in William Terrington's *Cooling Cups and Dainty Drinks* (1869) and in *Jayne's Bartender's Guide* (circa 1933) listing the ingredients as:

American Stoughton's Bitters
[William Terrington's version]
16 oz [453 gr] gentian root
12 oz [340 gr] orange-peel
3 oz [85 gr] Virginia snake-root
1 [28 gr] oz saffron
1 oz [28 gr] red saunders wood
Grind ingredients into a powder. Add

1 [imperial] gallon [1.2 US gallons] rectified spirit. Macerate for 3 weeks, constantly agitating for a fortnight. Strain carefully. The last pint of liquor strain separately with pressure. When it runs clear, add it to the clear spirit.

American Stoughton's Bitters
[Jayne's version]
4 oz [113 gr] orange peel
4 oz [113 gr] colombo
4 oz [113 gr] gentian
4 oz [113 gr] chamomile flowers
4 oz [113 gr] quassia
1 lb [454 gr] caramel
2.5 gallons [9.5 litres] whisky
Let it macerate for 4 to 5 weeks then strain and filter.

During the 1770s, two scientific discoveries led to the development of a product that became a mainstay in beverage culture: soda water.

Sparkling water. Fizzy water. Seltzer. Soda water. Call it what you will. Carbonated water has been a mainstay of the beverage industry ever since Selters spring, near the town of Neiderselters, was first discovered in 772 and documented. The health benefits of this bubbly, acidic water described by physician Jakob Theodor Tabernaemontanus, in 1581, set the wheels in motion for the development of a spa, where neighbouring residents, health-conscious gentry and even royalty could "take the waters."

A century later, a profitable enterprise in bottling and shipping "Selters Waters" in tightly-corked earthenware jugs to Scandinavia, Eastern Europe, North America and even the Dutch East Indies assured this town of 800 inhabitants a steady source of income beyond the flourishing tourism. Pricey and not always easy to come by, carbonated water became the Holy Grail for two scientists in precisely the same year.

Hoping to cure his digestive ailments without bearing the cost of importing sparkling water, a sickly but frugal Swedish chemistry professor named Torbern Bergman, in 1771, invented a process that replicated sparkling spring water using carbon dioxide gas generated from chalk and sulfuric acid dissolved in water.

Independently, that same year, British clergyman Joseph Priestley also discovered a method when he suspended a bowl of water above a beer vat at a brewery in Leeds. It had a pleasant taste and mouthfeel and he offered it to his friends. The next year,

Priestley published a paper entitled Impregnating Water with Fixed Air. Not particularly interested in financial gain from his thinking, Priestley never commercialised his discovery.

That step was left to Swiss watchmaker Jean-Jacob Schweppe, who read both of these accounts and conducted his own experiments. An epiphany occurred when he read, in 1777, that French chemist Antoine Lavoisier had determined that gas could be dissolved in water.

In 1783, Schweppe's discovery became a reality, when he wrote: "I use a compression pump which I named the 'Geneva Machine' because of my origins. In a stirring apparatus, I produce gas with chalk and sulfuric acid; I then purify it with water before heating it with a container full of charcoal. ...The taste is pretty strong. Maybe I should add natural plant oil."

More interested in gaining certification from the medical community than a profit, Schweppe unfortunately trusted the sales of his water to a friend, who commissioned engineer Nicolas Paul to fashion an aeration device to go into direct competition. Schweppe's water was exceeding the sales of Selter and other spa waters, so it was not surprising that a greedy rivalry emerged.

The tables turned when Paul made Schweppe's friend a substandard machine and himself a refined one. Better to join the enemy than fight. In 1790, Schweppe went into partnership with Paul and pharmacist Henry Albert Gosse, another experimenter with carbonated waters. The company of Schweppe, Paul and Gosse decided to make its product with distilled water as well as expand its offerings and operations to London.

From their first factory at 141 Drury Lane, the partnership produced three waters. In a letter between industrialist Matthew Boulton and natural philosopher Erasmus Darwin (grandfather of Charles Darwin) it was noted that "J. Schweppe prepares his mineral waters of three sorts. No. 1 is for common drinking with your dinner. No. 2 is for nephritic patients and No. 3 contains the most alkali given only in more violent cases."

The secret to Schweppe's success was its bottles. Gas commonly escaped around the cork leaving carbonated water flat within a day. The company packaged its waters in strong stoneware bottles with a rounded bottom that required it to be stored on its side, a position that kept the cork wet. Schweppe's sparkling water sold for at apothecaries 6s, 6d per dozen, including the bottles.

Pressure from his partners to return to Geneva coupled with an expensive attempt to construct cheap mineral water machines to encourage street cart sales fueled the 1795 dissolution of the company. But it did not deter the inventor. Moving first to 8 Kings Street in Holborn and then to 11 Margaret Street In Cavendish Square, he continued to build his Schweppe Company with the growing support of the British medical community and the public at large.

In his late fifties, Schweppe saw the end of the eighteenth century as a wealthy entrepreneur. He had made a considerable profit and decided to retire, in 1798, selling 75% of his interest to three Channel island businessmen: Henry William Lauzun, Francis Charles Lauzun and Robert Charles Brohier. Although he and his wife Charlotte returned to Switzerland the following year, his Schweppe Company found itself on the brink of rising to even greater heights in the hands of its new owners.

Popular lore tells us that a few years after Schweppe's soda water became the toast of London, John (or Jim) Collins – headwaiter at Limmer's Hotel & Coffee House on Conduit Street – created a drink that became known as the John Collins. Sung to the tune of "Jenny Jones," this ditty, appearing in the 8 August 1891 issue of Punch, praised Collins' libations:

> My name in JIM COLLINS,
> 'Ead-vaiter at Limmers',
> The corner of Conduck Street,
> 'Anover Square.
> And my hokkipashun
> Is sarvin' out liquors
> To such sportin' covies
> As chance to come there.

John Collins

2 oz [60 ml] genever
1 oz [30 ml] fresh lemon juice
3 barspoons caster sugar
Build ingredients into a collins glass over crushed ice and churn. Top with soda water. Finish with another topping of crushed ice. Garnish with 2 lemon slices and serve with 2 straws.

As we mentioned earlier, the infusion of wormwood into wine hails from ancient Chinese and Greco-Roman times. Wine fortification via the mutage process dates back to the 1200s and Arnaud de Ville-Neuve. In 1786, a product that incorporated both processes was born in a liquor shop below the porticoes of the Piazza della Fiera (now Piazza Castello) on the corner with Via della Palma (now Via Viotti) in Torino, Italy.

Signor Marendazzo hired a helper named Antonio Benedetto Carpano (1765–1815), who moved from Bioglio Biellese. Carpano had it in his mind to create an aromatic wine from moscato, based on a recipe made by the monks in his native valley. The 22-year-old apprentice macerated more than 30 spices and herbs, including wormwood, into the sweet wine. Then he fortified it with distilled spirit.

Marendazzo let him sell it in the shop. The drink became an immediate hit. Popular lore tells us that Carpano had a passion for Goethe's poetry and named his new drink after the German word for wormwood, *wermut* (pronounced "ver-moot"). The term had been in use since at least the early 1600s in Austria, Hungary and other neighbouring countries as the name of an aromatised bitter wine.

Popular lore also tells us that a basket of Carpano's new product was sent to the

Duke of Savoy Vittorio Amedeo III, who found it so exquisite, he suspended the production of the court's rosolio (a type of sweet liqueur made from roses and spices) and ordered cases of Carpano's vermouth instead.

A quick historical note: As a child, Vittorio was very frail and the royal doctor suggested the family find new foods to improve his appetite. Grissini (the thin breadsticks served all over Torino) were developed for the young prince, helping him put on weight and soon became a resounding success with aristocrats.

Torinese café society may have emerged, in 1763, with the opening of Al Bicerin Café in Torino's Piazza della Consolata. The place was known for a frothy blend of espresso and chocolate since its opening. But it was Carpano's vermouth that solidified the city's tradition of *aperitivo* when his shop was converted into a café that was open 24 hours a day.

There is one earlier story of the birth of vermouth that was brought to our attention by mixologist Agostino Perrone. Long before Antonio Carpano was born, another Antonio is reputed to have entered the aromatized wine business:

Antonio Cinzano. He was allegedly recognized as the owner of a shop, in 1568, that produced a wine-based drink. His descendants Carlo Stefano Cinzano and his brother Giovanni Giacomo became licencees, in 1757, in the deeds of the prestigious "University of Confectioners and Spirit Manufacturers" of Torino. It is said that the Cinzano brothers relocated the family business – which included an herb shop – to Via Dora Cassa that same year. We have not been able to substantiate this history to the extent that we did with the Carpano story. So this point remains unresolved at the time of this writing.

What we do know is that much like the provenance of genever, the birth of vermouth can be traced to Hippocrates' recipe for a wormwood and dittany infusion into wine, *vinum Hippocraticum*. The name Hippocras or Ypocras eventually evolved into a term used to describe any number of recipes that involved the infusion of herbs and spices into wine that were meant to be served as digestifs after a heavy meal.

During the 1550s, the pairing of wormwood and wine reappeared in German and Italian monastic recipes for another digestive tonic, *vinum absinthum*. These were probably the source and inspiration for both Carpano and Cinzano.

There is also a bit of a dispute over the originator of another wormwood-based spirit: absinthe. Some historians declare that Dr Pierre Ordinaire, an exiled French royalist living in Switzerland, created *la fée verte* [the green fairy] in 1792 as a distilled elixir. Others say Ordinaire stole the recipe from the Henriod sisters from Couvet, who advertised their *extrait d'absinthe*, around 1769, in a Neuchâtel newspaper. And both sides claim that Major Daniel-Henri Dubied purchased the recipe from one of the parties by 1792. Enough of what historians have to say.

What is known is that around 1794, a Couvet-based distiller named Abram-Louis Perrenoud scribbled in his diary a recipe for *extrait d'absinthe*. Major Dubied purchased Perrenoud's recipe and employed the distiller's son Henri-Louis to produce the formula, which they did four years later along with Dubied's sons under the name Dubied Père et Fils. The relationship lasted for about seven years.

Then Henri-Louis Perrenoud changed his surname to Pernod and established

his own absinthe distillery: Pernod Fils. The company continued making the product until absinthe was banned in the 1910s, after becoming the spirit of choice for the high-born, the low-born and everyone in between.

Bitters, soda water, vermouth, absinthe, two new forms of whiskey, merged with an audience that craved spirits, sugar and anything new: The stage was set for an exciting event that took place back in the northeastern United States, in a tavern.

CHAPTER SEVEN
Taverns, Inns & Café Society

THE EMERGENCE OF MIXED DRINKS IN THE AMERICAN STYLE

Does it really come as a surprise that the earliest documented tavern was located in Sumer around 3500 BC? The region was an arid flood plain that required sophisticated irrigation techniques to cultivate even the hardiest grain. Beverages came no easier for the residents. However, the locals were a pretty smart lot. They spoke Akkadian. But officials and nobles also read and wrote Sumerian. They even documented the existence of drinking establishments in the kingdom. Lucky for us.

In this area, which is now part of Iraq, there had to be some reward for the average person toiling in the dry, burning sun day after day. The tavern was it. A bastion of male bonding, women were allowed to work in and even run taverns, but were forbidden to frequent them. It gave men a place to go after a hard day's tilling, to get away from the drudgery of family life and to gossip over the latest war or conquest. It was a home away from home.

Surely word spread at the taverns that Sumer had been conquered and incorporated into the empire of Babylon around 1780BC along with neighbouring Akkad. What they didn't realize was that their new king, Hammurabi, knew about the taverns. He included two rules concerning them in his Codex of 282 laws. To ensure obedience, he blamed the laws on the gods and warned the people of all sorts of curses that might befall them along with corporal punishments meted out by officials and the military.

Woe betide the female tavern-keeper if, according to Law 108, she "does not accept corn according to gross weight in payment of drink, but takes money and the price of the drink is less than that of the corn, she shall be convicted and thrown into the water."

And shame on her if, according to Law 109, "conspirators meet in the house of a tavern-keeper and these conspirators are not captured and delivered to the court, the tavern-keeper shall be put to death."

No one could say they never heard of the Codex, a stone stela of it was placed in the centre of town and there was always someone who could read it to the people for whom it applied. Hammurabi also came up with the concept that a person must be considered innocent until guilt is proven.

The ritual of going to the tavern continued pretty much status quo and unabated. For a time, taverns fell into disrepute. Among ancient Greeks, these venues were on par with hostels in today's parlance. Keepers were not generally trusted with personal property after having served a hapless guest a fair share of second-rate drink and third-rate food before sending him off to a flea-ridden bed. Most travellers relied on lodgings with friends rather than enter the door of a *taberna* [inn].

The Romans faced similar conditions. Under their laws, the keeper of a place such as the Three Taverns on the Appian Way was responsible for a patron's property unless the damage was caused by *damnum fatale* [act of God] or *vis major* [the emperor's enemies]. The owner was also liable for damage done by a servant, slave or other household member. This code of conduct followed the Romans across the English Channel.

London's drinking heritage dates back to 43AD when the Romans invaded Britain. As troops advanced northward from their landing in Kent, they were halted by the River Thames. Leader Aulus Plautius ordered a bridge to be built and then a settlement called Londinium, which quickly became the central trading centre between Britain and the rest of the Roman Empire.

You can probably blame the Romans for importing the tavern and its law of innkeepers to British shores. Although taverns were, at first, considered a scant second when compared to staying with friends or family on a journey from one end of the empire to the other, these simple hostelries offered weary travellers food, drink, rest from the road and a place to exchange ideas. Fortunately, the tavern doors did not close when the mighty empire withdrew from Britain in the fifth century. In fact, taverns improved in the hands of the Britons. By the time Geoffrey Chaucer wrote about the Tabard and Checquers of the Hope in his *Canterbury Tales* in the thirteenth century, the mobile merchant class favoured these havens over the meagre environs of monasteries and hospices.

Just like their Sumerian predecessors, many keepers of these wayfarer havens were women, known as ale-wives because the most common fare served was beer. The Tabard, the Ship and Turtle and the Bear were the only taverns in London until 1552 when an act allowed 40 houses to open in the city in addition to the hundreds and hundreds that sprouted up throughout the country.

How popular did taverns become? As Henry C Shelley wrote in his 1909 book *Inns and Taverns of Old London*:

> *For all races of Teutonic origin the claim is made that they are essentially home-loving people. Yet the Englishman of the sixteenth and seventeenth and eighteenth centuries, especially of the latter, is seen to have exercised considerable zeal in creating substitutes for that home which, as a Teuton, he ought to have loved above all else.*

The social nature of the tavern didn't change much, apart from the name, when the Puritans made their way to American shores in 1620 to escape religious oppression. Though commonly portrayed in history books as teetotallers, the Puritans brought *aqua vitae* [brandy] and "strong waters" [Holland gin or Plymouth gin], which they consumed at lunch on board the *Mayflower*. The Pilgrims landed in Plymouth, Massachusetts, because their shipboard stores of beer ran out. They shared their strong waters with chief Massasoit of the Wampanoags on his first visit to the colony. They called their taverns by a new name: ordinaries. (This name referred to the fixed-price meals they offered and soon came to refer to the establishments that offered them as well [from the Middle English *ordinaire*, which came from Old French].)

Plymouth was not the only point of encounter for indigenous North Americans, European colonists and their spirits. Even before the Pilgrims landed, British explorer Henry Hudson shared a social tipple with the locals. Commissioned by the Muscovy Company of England, in 1607, Hudson set sail to locate and plot the fabled Northwest Passage to Asia. He failed to find it. He made a second attempt, in 1608, trying to go across the top of Russia. That too, was an unsuccessful mission. Based on reports of the establishment of the Jamestown Colony by Captain John Smith, the Dutch East India Company asked Hudson, in 1609, to chart a Southwest Passage to Asia.

Sailing on board the *Halve Maen* [Half Moon], Hudson's expedition made landfall on an island where they encountered Delaware tribesmen. In hopes of establishing friendly relations, Hudson offered the tribal chief some brandy, which after tasting it, the leader soon fell asleep. The next morning, the chief requested sample sips for the rest of his party. After Hudson departed, the Delawares called the island *"Manahachtanienk"* [the place where we got high]. Thus, today, the island is known as Manhattan.

It took a few years for the colonists to settle into their new surroundings. First, they discovered British grain didn't fair well in the harsh New England climate. So much for making beer.

They resorted to fermenting hard cider from whatever they could find: apples, pears, you name it. When twenty ships delivered more than 20,000 new colonists over the course of a couple of years, they also off-loaded more brandy, gin and rum. The need for congenial meeting places grew. Samuel Cole opened, in 1634, Boston's first ordinary.

New England ordinaries were among the most highly regulated enterprises in the colonies. Keepers were certified by local selectmen as being honourable men and licenced by county officials. An owner could be prosecuted for "refusing to make suitable provision when desired, for the receiving of strangers, travellers or others and their horses and cattle, or for any public entertainment"; if convicted, he lost his licence and had his sign taken down by the sheriff.

On Sunday, owners had to turn away new guests and locals; they only could feed and lodge travellers who had already checked in. This is ironic, since ordinaries were meant for the townspeople to enjoy and were engaged in accommodating wayfarers.

Tavern-keepers spent most of their time being hotel clerks, food servers and pourers leaving them little time or reason to become skilled barmen. But they were busy behind the bar.

A TALE OF THE COCKTAIL

Historian dave Wondrich uncovered the clue to the greatest beverage invention of the 1700s in New York State, where Thomas and Catherine Hustler kept a tavern, between 1776 and 1783, at

Storm's Bridge (now called Elmsford, New York). The tavern was positioned on the Post Road that connected New York and Albany: a bustling thoroughfare in those early days. But it wasn't until the Hustlers moved in 1809 and opened another establishment in Lewiston in Upstate New York, that any one documented just what Catherine Hustler had created during the American Revolution – the Cocktail.

Around 1820, author James Fenimore Cooper (1789–1851) stayed at the couple's tavern, while writing his second novel *The Spy: A Tale of Neutral Ground*. In it, he featured a character named Betty Flanagan, who Cooper based on Catherine Hustler's reminiscences of those tumultuous times. In one passage he wrote:

Her faults were, a trifling love of liquor, excessive filthiness and a total disregard of all the decencies of language; her virtues, an unbounded love for her adopted country, perfect honesty when dealing on certain known principles with the soldiery and great good nature. Added to these, Betty had the merit of being the inventor of that beverage which is so well known, at the present hour, to all the patriots who make a winter's

march between the commercial and political capitals of this great state, and which is distinguished by the name of 'cocktail.' Elizabeth Flanagan was peculiarly well qualified, by education and circumstances, to perfect this improvement in liquors, having been literally brought up on its principal ingredient, and having acquired from her Virginian customers the use of mint, from its flavour in a julep to its height of renown in the article in question.

Before Cooper documented the word "cocktail," the term appeared, in 1803, in a small newspaper published in Amherst, New Hampshire. Wondrich uncovered the word's earliest appearance in print in a little humour article purported to come from the diary of a "lounger" in the 28 April edition of the *Farmer's Cabinet*, which read:

11. Drank a glass of coctail – excellent for the head … Call'd at the Doct's. found Burnham – he looked very wise – drank another glass of cocktail.

As the eighteenth century gave way to the nineteenth century, tavern life was one of the few constants. For the most part the 1830 edition of the *American Encyclopedia* pretty much summed up the period by noting that:

A fashion at the South was to take a glass of whiskey, flavoured with mint, soon after waking; and so conducive to health was this nostrum esteemed that no sex, and scarcely any age, were deemed exempt from its application. At eleven o'clock, while mixtures, under various peculiar names-sling, toddy, flip, etc.-solicited the appetite at the bar of the common tippling-shop, the offices of professional men and counting rooms dismissed their occupants for a half hour to regale themselves at a neighbor's or a coffee-house with punch, hot or cold, according to the season; and females or valetudinarians, courted an appetite with medicated rum, disguised under the chaste names of 'Hexham's Tinctures' or 'Stoughton's Elixir.' The dinner hour arrived…whiskey and water curiously flavoured with apples, or brandy and water, introduced the feast; whiskey or brandy and water helped it through; and whiskey or brandy without water secured its safe digestion, not to be used in any more formal manner than for the relief of occasional thirst or for the entertainment of a friend, until the last appeal should be made to them to secure a sound night's sleep. Rum, seasoned with cherries, protected against the cold; rum, made astringent with peach-nuts, concluded the repast at the confectioner's; rum, made nutritious with milk, prepared for the maternal office. … No doubt there were numbers who did not use ardent spirits, but it was not because they were not perpetually in their way. … The friend who did not testify his welcome, and the employer who did not provide bountifully of them for his help, was held niggardly, and there was no special meeting, not even of the most formal or sacred kind, where it was considered indecorous, scarcely any place where it was not thought necessary, to produce them…

Politicians had fully adopted the tradition of campaigning for office with a healthy dose of spirits proffered at a local tavern. Case in point: A satirical item that appeared in the 6 May 1806 edition of *The Balance and Columbian Repository*, published by Harry Croswell in Hudson, New York. It mentioned that a certain Democratic-Republican candidate (today he would have been known as a Republican candidate) had spent a hefty sum on 720 rum-grogs, 17 dollars brandy, 32 gin-slings, 411 glasses bitters and 25 dollars on cocktails. The candidate's gain? Nothing. He lost the election.

During the week a subscriber wrote:

Sir,

I observe in your paper of the 6th instant, in the account of a democratic candidate for a seat in the legislature, marked under the head of Loss, 25 dollars cock-tail. Will you be so obliging as to inform me what is meant by this species of refreshment? Though a stranger to you, I believe, from your general character, you will not suppose this request to be impertinent.

I have heard of a jorum, of phlegm-cutter and fog driver, of wetting the whistle, or moistening the clay, of a fillip, a spur in the head, quenching the spark in the head, of slip, etc., but never in my life, though I have lived a good many years, did I hear of cock-tail before. Is it peculiar to this part of the country? Or is it a late invention? Is the name expressive of the effect which the drink has on a particular part of the body? Or does it signify that the democrats who take the potion are turned topsy-turvy, and have their heads where their tails should be? I should think the latter to be the real solution; but am unwilling to determine finally until I receive all the information in my power....

Yours,

A SUBSCRIBER"

Croswell replied thus:

[As I make it a point, never to publish anything (under my editorial head) but which I can explain, I shall not hesitate to gratify the curiosity of my inquisitive correspondent: Cock tail, then is a stimulating liquor, composed of spirits of any kind, sugar, water and bitters it is vulgarly called a bittered sling, and is supposed to be an excellent electioneering potion inasmuch as it renders the heart stout and bold, at the same time that it fuddles the head. It is said also, to be of great use to a democratic candidate: because, a person having swallowed a glass of it, is ready to swallow any thing else.

Edit. Bal.]

This raised a certain level of curiosity up and down the Post Road that stretched from New York to Albany. Word must have spread pretty fast. In his 1809 multi-volume *Knickerbocker's History of New York*, Washington Irving (1783–1859) criticized the citizens of the state of Maryland for claiming to have invented the cocktail in their fair state rather than his New York birthplace scoffing that:

These gigantic savages and smokers caused no little disquiet in the mind of Mynheer Beekman, threatening to cause a famine of tobacco in the land; but his most formidable enemy was the roaring, roistering English colony of Maryland, or, as it was anciently written, Merryland; so called because the inhabitants, not having the fear of the Lord before their eyes, were prone to make merry and get fuddled with mint-julep and apple-toddy. They were, moreover, great horse-racers and cock-fighters, mighty wrestlers and jumpers, and enormous consumers of hoe-cake and bacon. They lay claim to be the first inventors of those recondite beverages, cock-tail, stone-fence, and sherry-cobbler, and to have discovered the gastronomical merits of terrapins, soft crabs, and canvas-back ducks.

New York City had grown by fits and bounds before its first hotel was built in 1806 on the site of the old De Lancey House at the corner of Broadway and Cedar Street: the City Hotel. As Edwin S Burrows and Mike Wallace wrote in their 1998 book, *Gotham: A History of New York City to 1898*:

So many transients arrived, for business as well as pleasure, that taverns and boardinghouses proved unable to accommodate the influx. This dilemma led to the construction of New York's first hotel in the modern sense-the five story 137-room City Hotel....Besides room and board, it offered the facilities for public dining and dancing hitherto provided by taverns. Its gracious accommodations and excellent wine cellars were specifically designed to attract a wealthy clientele, and its "very handsome" street-level shops, elegant barroom, and coffeehouse fronting Broadway became important mercantile gathering spots.

An "elegant barroom". Instead of a tavern-keeper or an innkeeper serving up a mixed drink, a bartender strictly dedicated to serving drinks stood at duty. Initially, places like the City Hotel situated the bar in the lobby. In 1834, New York's first luxury hotel – the Astor House Hotel at 225 Broadway at Park Row – became the preeminent watering hole. Its early guest roster included United States President Andrew Jackson, Davy Crockett, Daniel Webster and Congressman Henry Clay. Trade was extremely brisk at hotel bars. As George Moore wrote in *Journal of a Voyage Across the Atlantic: with Notes on Canada & the United States and Return to Great Britain in 1844*:

We passed Washington Hall, where

many a fine fellow has been ruined by gaming and drinking; and dined at Astor House, where I was told it for a positive fact they take 500 dollars a day ready money for drinks of brandy by people standing. They pay 40,000 dollars a year rent.

While a guest checked in, a drink could be ordered from the desk clerk in the same manner taverns and inns handled the procedure. Making a drink was still simple in those early years: The mixer continued to stir the drink in a small tumbler with a toddy stick and served it to the customer, adding a little grating of nutmeg if so desired – just like his predecessors. Carryovers from the previous century, Punches, Slings, Grogs and Toddys were still the common calls.

Oxford Punch

"Extract the juice from the rind of these lemons, by rubbing loaf sugar on it. The peeling of two Seville oranges and two lemons, cut extremely thin. The juice of four Seville oranges and ten lemons. Six glasses of calves feet jelly in a liquid state. The above to be put into a jug and stirred well together. Pour two quarts of boiling water on the mixture, cover the jug closely and place it near the fire for a quarter of an hour. Then strain the liquid through a sieve into a punch bowl or jug, sweeten it with a bottle of capillaire and add half a pint of white wine, a pint of French brandy, a pint of Jamaica rum and a bottle of orange shrub; the mixture to be stirred as the spirits are poured in. In for sufficiently sweet, add loaf sugar gradually in small quantities or a spoonful or two of capillaire. To be served up either hot or cold."

Apple Toddy
1 baked apple
2 teaspoons sugar
1 wineglass [8 oz / 240 ml] applejack
Place the baked apple, sugar and applejack into a glass or mug. Fill two-thirds full with boiling water. Garnish with a little grated nutmeg.

In London, hotels and particularly hotel bars were already places where customers relied on the barkeeper's and the hotel's reputation, enough so that in the 22 April 1790 edition of *The Times*, a reader in the personals columns wrote: "The VOLUNTEER acknowledges the compliment paid by A.B. If [he] has any thing particular to communicate relating to the subject at hand, he will please to leave it at the Bar of the York Hotel [on New Bridge Street in Blackfriars]."

Birthplace of the John Collins, Limmer's Hotel & Coffee House on Conduit Street had a reputation by then, according to Edward Wadford in his 1878 book *Old and new London*, as "the most dirty hotel in London; but in the gloomy, comfortless coffee-room might be seen many members of the rich squirearchy, who visited London during the sporting season. This hotel was frequently so crowded that a bed could not be had for any amount of money; but you could always get a good plain English dinner, an excellent bottle of port, and some famous gin-punch." And who could resist the establishment's signature quaff, the John Collins or its siblings, the Tom Collins (made with Old Tom gin) and the Gin Fizz?

As British legislation changed, gin shops, dram shops and chemist's shops that dispensed gin mostly to take away or to drink standing up were replaced not only by hotel bars but by larger, licenced establishments. During the late 1820s, the city's first gin palaces arose: Thompson & Fearon's on Holborn and Weller's on Old Street. Garishly decorated, Charles Dickens (1812–1870) described the gin palaces in his 1836 book *Sketches by Boz*:

All is light and brilliancy. The hum of many voices issues from that splendid gin-shop which forms the commencement of the two streets opposite; and the gay building with the fantastically ornamented parapet, the illuminated clock, the plate-glass windows surrounded by stucco rosettes, and its profusion of gas-lights in richly-gilt burners, is perfectly dazzling when contrasted with the darkness and dirt we have just left.

The interior is even gayer than the exterior. A bar of French-polished mahogany, elegantly carved, extends the whole width of the place; and there are two side-aisles of great casks, painted green and gold, enclosed within a light brass rail, and bearing such inscriptions, as 'Old Tom, 549;' 'Young Tom, 360;' 'Samson, 1421'-the figures agreeing, we presume, with 'gallons,' understood. Beyond the bar is a lofty and spacious saloon, full of the same enticing vessels, with a gallery running round it, equally well furnished.

On the counter, in addition to the usual spirit apparatus, are two or three little baskets of cakes and biscuits, which are carefully secured at top with wicker-work, to prevent their contents being unlawfully abstracted. Behind it, are two showily-dressed damsels with large necklaces, dispensing the spirits and 'compounds.' They are assisted by the ostensible proprietor of the concern, a stout, coarse fellow in a fur cap, put on very much on one side to give him a knowing air, and to display his sandy whiskers to the best advantage

The gin palace's design became the template for the building of nineteenth-century public houses, adding beer engines to the efficient bar design as well as special touches such as mirrors and etched glass in a world that had little flourish for working class and the poor. The Princess Louise on High Holborn, The Red Lion on Duke of York Street, Princess Victoria on Uxbridge Road, Salisbury Pub on St Martin's Lane and The Argyll Arms on Argyll Street are some of the last remaining relatively-untouched establishments in this genre.

MISTER PIMM'S CUP

Lunchtime quaffers could quench their thirst at London's many oyster bars. A shellfish monger from Newnham, Kent named James Pimm (1798–1866) served up a unique "house cup" to accompany the seafood he served in Pimm's Oyster Bar, which opened in 1823 around Billingsgate, London. Shortly after he opened, Pimm blended gin, quinine and other herbs, fruits and

spices to pair with his shellfish, and began to serve it in a metal tankard marked with "No. 1" shortly after he opened. His primary patrons were the gentlemen who worked at the nearby Bank of England, Lloyds of London and the Stock Exchange. (Cups were a favourite with those who attended hunting parties on country estates during their weekends away from wheeling and dealing city business.) Obviously, Pimm did well for himself, opening another four oyster bars and commercially bottling his house cup by 1859 with the help of his patron-investors.

Pimm's Cup

*1 part Pimm's No. 1 Cup
3 parts sparkling lemonade
borage leaves
mint leaves
slices of orange, lemon and
    strawberry*
Built Pimm's and lemonade in a
    tumbler filled with ice. Garnish with
    borage leaves, mint leaves orange
    lemon, strawberry. (Note: Because
    borage leaves are not commonly
    available, a cucumber wedge is
    frequently substituted.)

Plymouth Fruit Cup

[Mixologist Wayne Collins was asked
    to replicate Pimm's No. 1 Cup a
    few years ago. This recipe was the

result, effectively reproducing the recipe from scratch as Mr Pimm himself must have done for years.]

1.5 oz [45 ml] Plymouth gin
1 oz [30 ml] Italian vermouth
0.5 oz [15 ml] Cointreau
0.5 oz [15 ml] maraschino liqueur
2 dashes Angostura bitters
Combine all ingredients in a glass over ice. Stir for 30 seconds.

GOD BLESS US, EVERYONE!

Gentlemen's clubs were another libational haven. A gathering place for men of like minds and interests, these members-only venues offered a range of specialities from Punches to Sangarees. Charles Dickens was a member of The Garrick Club, a group dedicated to the theatrical arts, which opened in 1831. The club's Summer Gin Punch was Dickens' favourite.

SUMMER GIN PUNCH

[Mixologist Charles Vexenat was asked to replicate The Garrick Club's famed Summer Gin Punch. This recipe was the result.]
1.25 oz [40 ml] London dry gin
1 splash [10 ml] maraschino liqueur
1 splash [10 ml] water
2 dashes [5 ml] gomme syrup
2 dashes [5 ml] fresh lemon juice
1 splash [10 ml] fresh orange juice
1 lemon twist
1 orange twist
2 fresh raspberries
2 chunks of diced pineapple
1 oz [25 ml] soda
Build all ingredients in a mixing glass over ice. Then transfer contents into a punch cup.

He generally seemed to enjoy a good cup of Punch and even featured the making of a Hot Gin Punch by Bob Crachit in his 1843 book, *A Christmas Carol*:

…back came Tiny Tim before another word was spoken, escorted by his brother and sister to his stool beside the fire; and while Bob, turning up his cuffs – as if, poor fellow, they were capable of being made more shabby – compounded some hot mixture in a jug with gin and lemons, and stirred it round and round, and put it on the hob to simmer, Master Peter and the two ubiquitous young Cratchits went to fetch the goose, with which they soon returned in high procession."

…At last the dinner was all done, the cloth was cleared, the hearth swept, and the fire made up. The compound in the jug being tasted, and considered perfect, apples and oranges were put upon the table, and a shovel full of chestnuts on the fire.

Then all the Cratchit family drew round the hearth in what Bob Cratchit called a circle, meaning half a one; and at Bob Cratchit's elbow stood the family display of glass. Two tumblers and a custard cup without a handle.

These held the hot stuff from the jug, however, as well as golden goblets would have done; and Bob served it out with beaming looks, while the chestnuts on the fire sputtered and cracked noisily. Then Bob proposed:

"A merry Christmas to us all, my dears. God bless us!"

Which all the family re-echoed.

"God bless us every one!" said Tiny Tim, the last of all.

HOT GIN PUNCH RECIPE

[We were asked to create a version of Bob Cratchit's Hot Gin Punch for Christmas 2007. This was the result.]
1 dried lemon peel
1 dried orange peel
20 whole dry cloves
0.5 tsp coriander seeds
1 tsp Anardana (pomegranate seeds)
10 Elaichi (green cardamom pods)
10 dried juniper berries
2 two-inch pieces of Dalcini or Ceylonese cinnamon bark
1 pint water
Simmer all ingredients in a saucepan for 5 minutes. In a tea cup, add 50 ml London dry gin. Add hot liquid mixture. Top with ginger beer.

For those who could not afford to walk into hotel bars, oyster bars, gentlemen's clubs or gin palaces, there was always someone purveying a refreshing shrub (derived from the Arabic word *sharab*, meaning "to drink"): the poor man's cocktail.

CITRUS SHRUB

Pour 2 quarts of brandy into a large bottle. Add the juice of 5 lemons, peels of 2 lemons and half a nutmeg. Seal it and let steep for 3 days. Add 3 pints of white wine and 1.5 lbs [680 gr] demerara sugar. Mix until dissolved. Strain the mixture twice through a filtering bag and then bottle it up.

Back in New York City, the drinking establishment also evolved. During the late 1700s and early 1800s, young New York gentlemen generally travelled out of the city proper for a bit of card-playing, cockfighting, raucous music and a quaff or two at "entertainment resorts" instead of making merry at Brom Martling's Long Room at Nassau and Spruce Streets where the respectable Society of St Tammany gents moved their quarters, nicknaming it "the Wigwam." Niblo's

Suburban Pleasure Ground was another favourite for evening outings.

But the afternoon spot was exceptional. A resort and coach stop on the old Harlem road became best known for the owner's Mint Juleps and Gin Cocktails.

Gin Cocktail
1 wineglass [4 oz / 120 ml]
  Holland gin
1 teaspoon sugar
2 dashes bitters
Place ingredients in a glass. Stir.
  Add a splash of water.

The lane on which his establishment was situated was even named after him and was situated from 1805 until 1853 on the old Brevoort estate, situated between Fifty-Fourth and Fifty-Fifth Streets near First Avenue in Manhattan. In his 1882 historical account of the old days in New York entitled *Last Days of Knickerbocker Life in New York*, Abram C Dayton recounted that:

Cato's Lane…was one of the spurting sports on the drive. It was a semi-circular road about three-quarters of a mile in length, leading from Third Avenue, and again meeting it at a point not far distant from the sport on which now stands the Third Avenue Railroad Depot at Sixty-fifth Street.

Owned by Cato Alexander, Cato's Inn was where the cool crowd hung out on their way to and from bustling New York and to the country estates and mansions of Harlem that had grown out of a quiet farming community before the revolution. As Drayton described him:

This Cato was a famous man in his generation. A sable son of Africa, he lived and died respected in a community far more aristocratic and exclusive than its more pretentious democratic successors, yet it was unbiased by any tinge of modern abolition doctrine; a community which knew nothing of sensational issues. Cato was black, but long intimate contact with the gentlemen he served had imparted to his gentle, modest nature an unpretending dignity of manner, which won the esteem of all who approached him and secured for his humble house of entertainment such a widespread reputation, that for years it was one of the prominent resorts of our citizens, and attracted many of the prominent sight-seers who made the pilgrimages to the island of Manhattan.

Alexander was civic and politically minded. He was a founding member of the New York African Society for Mutual Relief, founded in 1808 but said to have met secretly as early as 1784. The group provided sickness and death benefits to its members at a time when insurance was not available to African-Americans.

During the War of 1812, Alexander placed an advertisement in the 17 August 1814 edition of the *New York Evening Post* that read:

> *The free coloured people of the 9th ward are requested to meet on Thursday evening the 17th inst. At 7 o'clock, at the house of Peter Stephens, near the 3-mile stone, on the Harlem Road, for the purpose of tendering their services to the committee of defence, in the erection of the fortifications at Brooklyn Heights."*

Shortly after the War of 1812, Edward Prime founded a foxhunting club, the Belvidere, that met at Cato's place. Mind you, Cato Alexander was indeed a rarity in New York City. Slavery was not abolished in New York State until 1828. Yet Alexander, Fraunces Tavern's owner Samuel Fraunces and Wall Street restaurateur Thomas Downing were three prosperous and influential free black men, 50 years before abolition became law.

SOMETHING SWEET

By all accounts, mint Juleps, like the ones made by Cato Alexander, were documented in print as far back as the 1790s. It is quite likely that the Julep was brought to the New World by French settlers, who first landed in Wisconsin in 1634 and colonized the area north of the Ohio River and east of the Mississippi, from western Pennsylvania to Illinois.

Although the word "julep" is derived from the Arabic *juleb*, the word "julep' itself is an old French or Provençale word that came from Latin as a term for a medicinal mixture containing no solids. It was still in use by pharmacists as late as 1915, appearing in British medical texts such as Peter McEwan's *The Art of Dispensing*. The transition from medicine to pleasure was a small step. The Brandy Julep was considered to be an excellent preventative against malaria, something French colonists would have imbibed in the swampy regions of Illinois, Missouri, Kentucky, Tennessee, Arkansas, Mississippi and Louisiana during the swelteringly humid summertime.

One of our favourite stories about the Julep's origins comes from Alexander Davidson and Bernard Stuve's 1876 book, A *Complete History of Illinois from 1673 to 1873*. In it, they narrate a story told by presidential-hopeful Stephen Douglas about George Rogers Clark, who led colonial troops from Pennsylvania down the Ohio River to stop the British from establishing a western front during the American Revolution. According to Douglas, Clark called out "Surrender you suckers, you" to French colonists living, in 1779, in Kaskaskia, Illinois. The settlers were allegedly sipping Mint Juleps through straws made from rye stalks when Clark and his men arrived. That, Douglas claimed, was the reason Illinois became affectionately called the "Sucker State."

Brother of William Clark, of Lewis and Clark expedition fame, George was ultimately responsible for securing the Northwest Territory for the United States and for founding Louisville, Kentucky. (The settlement was named after King Louis XVI of France, with whom the fledging nation had just signed an accord.)

BRANDY JULEP
2 teaspoons superfine sugar
1 oz [30 ml] still water
6 sprigs mint
3 oz [90 ml] cognac

Dissolve the sugar in the water in a highball glass. Add 3 mint sprigs and gently muddle them against the sides of the glass. Remove the sprigs and fill the glass with shaved ice and pour in the cognac. Add more ice and stir vigorously. Insert 3 sprigs of fresh mint and serve with a straw.

The word "sucker" and its relationship to a Julep resounded again in a 15 July 1860 passage in the *Brooklyn Daily Eagle*:

The Way to Take a Julep. – An exchange says: – Yesterday we saw a gorgeous youthful sucker imbibing a julep in the most luxurious style. Amid the green leaves of the mint reposed a full blown rose; and inhaled the fragrance of the flower, while he sucked up through a straw iced liquid with the most exquisite satisfaction.

The most famous documentation about the Mint Julep, comes from Captain Frederick Maryatt, who in his 1839 *Diary in America Series II, Volume I*, wrote:

But the Americans do not confine themselves to foreign wines or liquors; they have every variety at home, in the shape of compounds, such as mint-julep and its varieties; slings in all their varieties; cocktails, but I really cannot remember, or if I could, it would occupy too much time to mention the whole battle array against one's brains. I must, however, descant a little upon the mint-julep; as it is, with the thermometer at 100°, one of the most delightful and insinuating potations that ever was invented, and may be drank with equal satisfaction when the thermometer is as low as 70°. There are many varieties, such as those composed of Claret, Madeira, etcetera; but the ingredients of the real mint-julep are as follows. I learnt how to make them, and succeeded pretty well. Put into a tumbler about a dozen sprigs of the tender shoots of mint, upon them put a spoonful of white sugar, and equal proportions of peach and common brandy, so as to fill it up one third, or perhaps a little less. Then take rasped or pounded ice, and fill up the tumbler. Epicures rub the lips of the tumbler with a piece of fresh pine-apple, and the tumbler itself is very often incrusted outside with stalactites of ice. As the ice melts, you drink. I once overheard two ladies talking in the next room to me, and one of them said, "Well, we have a weakness for any one thing, it is for a mint-julep – "a very amiable weakness, and proving her good sense and good taste. They are, in fact, like the American ladies, irresistible.

The Virginians claim the merit of having invented this superb compound, but I must dispute it for my own country, although it has been forgotten of late. In the times of Charles the First and Second it must have been known, for Milton expressly refers to it in his Comus: –

*Behold the cordial julep – here
Which flames and dances in its crystal bounds
With spirits of balm and fragrant syrups mixed.
Not that Nepenthes, which the wife of Thone
In Egypt gave to Jove-born Helena
Is of such power to stir up joy like this,
To life so friendly, or so cool to thirst."*

If that don't mean mint-julep, I don't know the English language."

Rum, brandy, wine, whiskey, it made no difference what spirit was involved, Juleps were even more popular than cocktails during the first half of the 1800s. This passage from an article that appeared in the St Louis Reville and was reprinted in the 1848 *Brooklyn Daily Eagle* exemplifies the passion:

"What say you to the juleps, boys?" inquired Bill.

"Considering the state of the weather, we will go julep," said one of the guests;- "juleps all round."

"Hurrah for 'cooling drinks!'"echoed the whole party.

Sam, a negro servant, was summoned, and a positive order issued forthwith, for all the concomitants necessary to make a good julep. The brandy came, then the rum, the mint, fresh from the earth, then the sugar-

"Now, Sam, the ice," was the next call, and off started their attentive waiter. He soon returned with a towel full of the material, broken up fine, and in proper order, and now the revel began.

In the United States, Juleps were ubiquitous. According to historian Dave Wondrich, even the mysterious and celebrated Willard, who started at the City Hotel in lower Manhattan around 1815, gained a certain notoriety for his Juleps, in addition to his Extra Extra Peach Brandy Punch, Apple Toddys and his customer relations, "because Willard remembered their names."

Juleps and Cocktails. There is a fascinating association between the mint sprig and the Cocktail – not the Julep – that crept into cocktail lore during the mid-1800s and was recounted by an old New Yorker in the 17 October 1897 edition of the *Brooklyn Daily Eagle*:

But one day I heard the expression, 'Put a cocktail in it,' addressed to the barkeeper by a man who had ordered a sherry cobbler. The barkeeper took a single sprig of mint and stuck it into the ice of the cobbler on the opposite side from the straw. On speaking of the matter to an old friend, he said it had grown from a simple thing. A young man, taking a sherry cobbler, reached out, took a sprig of mint, stuck it into the cobbler and slowly sucked it through a straw and enjoyed the odor of the mint. As he put the glass down he remarked that the combination, straw, glass, and mint, looked like a game cock. It was one of those little things that 'catch on,' and the expression, 'put in a cocktail,' came to the front, meaning put in a sprig of mint, no matter what the drink. But it happened the drink into which it was oftenest put was the appetizer then usually spoken of as 'taking your bitters.' 'Your bitters,' with or without a 'cocktail' (sprig of mint) usually with, was 'the go.' The rest is easy-'Bitters with a cocktail,' 'cocktail bitters,' 'cocktail'-any spirit or wine with bitters in it....This was in effect the explanation given me thirty-five years ago in New York, when I first heard the expression, and until I read the article in your paper have always supposed it to be the true one.

To this day, no one has divined the truth of the Cocktail's origins, but this story seems to be one of the more plausible ones.

Our opinion of the Cocktail's origins goes back to the 1806 definition of the Cocktail as "...spirits of any kind, sugar, water and bitters – it is vulgarly called a bittered sling..." So, the difference between a Sling and a Cocktail was the addition of bitters. Early bitters dasher bottles were topped with a cork that had a short piece of feather shaft pushed through it to administer a dash of bitters when it was upturned. The feather would have likely been from a chicken, perhaps even a rooster. Thus, the difference between a sling and a cocktail was a dash through the cock's tail.

THE STRANGE CASE OF THE BATIDA

A chain of events changed the face of nineteenth-century Brazil and the rest of the world. Between 1807 and 1808, Napoléon Bonaparte successfully invaded Portugal and Spain during his campaign to build the French Empire. This triggered the Peninsular War, which pitted Spain, Portugal and Great Britain against France.

To safeguard the crown, Regent João, his mother Maria I (not so affectionately known as "Maria the Mad") and their royal court fled to Rio de Janeiro in 1808. João immediately put steps into motion to change Brazil's global status, by installing a royal treasury, the Bank of Brazil, a printing office, library, university, military academy and court of law. His royal highness's arrival also marked a major influx of higher-bred, cultured Europeans. The city's population doubled from 50,000 to 100,000 with the arrival of new Spanish, French and British middle-class professionals, scientists and artists.

Regent João decreed the end of Portugal's commercial monopoly on Brazil. The merchants could sell to whom they chose without restrictions. This did not, however, please the merchants in either Rio de Janeiro or Lisbon. So João made some concessions. He limited free trade to Belém, São Luis, Recife, Salvador and Rio de Janeiro. Trade among other colonial ports was reserved for Portuguese vessels. The tariff on imported goods, which had been 24 percent, was reduced to 16 percent for Portuguese imports.

Great Britain further attempted to

control the Brazilian market by signing the 1810 Treaty of Navigation and Commerce, which fixed a maximum tariff of fifteen percent on British textiles, hardware and earthenware imported into Brazil. This was followed by an 18 October 1810 decree that lowered duties on Portuguese imports from 16 to 15 percent. But this did not to restore Portuguese trade with Brazil. It essentially collapsed. Portugal, and consequently Brazil, could hardly protest at the time. Britain was instrumental in helping the Portuguese Crown regain its motherland from Napoléon and, at the time, Portuguese colonies were protected by British forces.

With the signing of the 1810 Treaty of Alliance and Friendship, the Crown agreed to limit slave trade in its own territories and vaguely promised to restrict its internal slave trade. (Five years later, this culminated in the signing of another treaty that ceased all slave trade north of the equator though in fact trade in human labour actually rose to its apex in the Americas around this time before subsiding in the 1820s.)

The new influx of middle-class Europeans and limitation of slave trade had two significant effects on cachaça production during the nineteenth century. A class rift between the new emigrants and the existing Brazilian population arose. Anything that was considered to be "Brazilian" was deemed lower class by the new arrivals, including cachaça consumption.

And with the reduction of the slave trade, the demand for cachaça – still exported to Africa under the name "jeritiba" – rapidly declined. Unlike rum, which enjoyed increased demand when the Royal Navy chose the spirit as its daily ration, cachaça did not gain British naval support despite Brazil's political ties.

The British naval blockades of sugar cane shipments to Europe during the Napoleonic Wars triggered interest in production of sugar from sugar beets in France, further decreasing the demand for Brazil's most successful export at that time.

Despite this shift in consumer perception, reports sent to the Crown from various travellers demonstrate that in rural areas, cachaça was still very much appreciated. In 1811, an advisor to Regent João, Monsignor Pizzaro reported that the village of Januária had 38 active plantations producing sugar and *aguardente de caña*. The French naturalist Auguste de Saint-Hilaire noted, in 1817, during his travels in the same area that sugar and cachaça were the first goods exchanged in trade swaps with locals.

Some historians believe that around this time the Batida, the Caipirinha's precursor, was invented by João's wife, Queen Carlota Joaquina. Portuguese historian Ana Roldão discovered documents showing large monthly orders of fruits and an average of eighty bottles of cachaça designated for not only the queen's apartments, but for those of the regent and other palace dwellers. Ice was not readily available in those days, so the royal Batidas were cooled on the outside of the serving vessels with a mixture of salt and ammonia.

Batida

2 oz [60 ml] cachaça
110 gr fruit juice or fruit pulp
1 barspoon simple syrup or superfine sugar
Shake vigorously all the ingredients in a shaker filled with ice. Pour the mixture unstrained into a collins glass.

Batidas, Juleps, Cocktails and other fancy drinks all needed one vital ingredient, aside from the alcohol: ice.

THE LITTLE ICE AGE

The end of an ice age launched the addition of ice to the cocktail recipe. The known world had not experienced an extended period of warm, constant seasonal temperatures since circa 1550, which marked the end of the Medieval Warm Period (800–1300) and the progression of the Little Ice Age (1400–1850) after the Atlantic pack ice began to grow around 1250. Warm summers became less dependable in Northern Europe around 1300, leading to the decline of the thriving British and German commercial vineyards by the 1400s.

The increasing number of cool, wet summers led to the Great Famine of 1315: no one thought of switching from grain crops that got battered in the winds and rains or rotted in storage, causing outbreaks of St. Anthony's Fire (ergot poisoning caused by the ingestion of mouldy rye flour) and malnutrition, a by-product of massive crop failures. The Black Death (1347–1351) was hastened because the population was starving and crowded in their huts with black rats carrying plague-ridden fleas. Believing cats to be agents of the Devil, they exterminated them and allowed the rats to live. Subsequent bubonic plague outbreaks in Italy (1629), London (1665), Vienna (1679), Marseille (1720) and Moscow (1771) show how long people refused to adapt to climactic change and the need for sound hygienic practices. (This was not the only time a population refused to accept change. The Irish Potato Famine of the nineteenth century was another established case of a population who starved because of successive crop failures triggered by severe climatic change, even though they were surrounded by the abundant sea life of the Atlantic Ocean.)

The world's great glaciers began a remarkable expansion around 1550 that lasted until 1850. Major river bodies froze over in winter: the Thames from 1607 to about 1806, New York Harbour in 1780, the Netherlands' rivers in 1794. Heightened volcanic activity caused atmospheric mayhem including 1816, the "year without summer."

The April 1815 eruption of Mount Tambora on Sumbawa Island in Indonesia was one of the worst volcanic explosions in recorded history, seconded only by the 27 August 1883 explosion of Krakatau in Indonesia's Sundra

Strait. Tambora became active in 1812 and culminated in an explosive central vent eruption with pyroclastic flows and collapse of the caldera. The eruption caused tsunamis and the deaths of more than 71,000 people. The eruptions and aftershocks continued until 15 July.

The founder of Singapore, Sir Thomas Stamford Bingley Raffles (1781–1826) recounted in his memoirs that:

The first explosions were heard on this Island in the evening of the 5th of April, they were noticed in every quarter, and continued at intervals until the following day. The noise was, in the first instance, almost universally attributed to distant cannon; so much so, that a detachment of troops were marched from Djocjocarta, in the expectation that a neighbouring post was attacked, and along the coast boats were in two instances dispatched in quest of a supposed ship in distress.

The Mount Tambora incident also caused a global climate anomaly. The following year, a persistent dry fog pervaded New England. It reddened and dimmed the sunlight. Sunspots were visible to the naked eye. Neither wind nor rainfall dispersed the "fog."

Average global temperatures decreased about 0.5 degrees Celsius, causing crop failures, the death of livestock and outbursts of typhus. On 4 June 1816, frost was reported in Connecticut. On 6 June, snow fell in Albany, New York and Dennysville, Maine. A 12-inch deep blizzard fell on Quebec City. Crop failures from temperature change caused severe famines in Wales, Ireland and Germany. It was the second coldest year recorded in Europe since 1400: the first was 1601 following the eruption of Huaynaputina in Peru.

With all this chilling environmental activity, cool drinks were not on people's minds. Far from it.

But just before the Little Ice Age came to an end, an engineer came up with a way for farmers to transport dairy products to market during the summer. In 1803, Thomas Moore invented the refrigerator so farmers in Maryland could deliver their butter to customers in sweltering Washington DC. It was a simple apparatus: A cedar tub lined with sheet metal was padded with rabbit fur and then packed with ice into which the butter was stored. The container was loaded onto a horse-driven cart and whisked down the road.

For the most part, only the well-to-do harvested ice, crushed it up, added flavourings and savoured it whenever and if ever the temperature rose. The Persians constructed yakhchals [ice storage] from around 400BC to store mountain ice harvested for royalty to enjoy in the hot desert summer. Roman- and later Italian-royalty did the same. Catherine de Medici introduced flavoured ices, in 1533, to the French court when she married King Henry II. One of her descendants, France's King Henry IV and his court fancied cooling his liqueurs and brandies with ice.

The first ice creams made with sweetened milk cooled with a mix of ice and salt appeared in Naples around 1664. The first dish of it in British history was served on the Feast of St. George at Windsor Castle in 1671 for King Charles II and his royal court. Wealthy colonial Americans brought their taste for the frozen confection to the New World around 1700.

Throughout all of this, ice was hard to get: People and horse-drawn carts climbed into the mountains and onto glaciers or braved walking on lakes and ponds, cleared piles of loose snow to reach below the hard pack, cut the ice with one-person hand axes and saws, raised it onto the ice, towed it down to straw-lined caves, dugouts, cellars or covered wells and hoped that the summer temperatures wouldn't rise too high.

In eighteenth-century New England and Canadian people had more than their fair share of ice, but little reason or expendable income to consume it. Thanks to a booming economy in tobacco, cotton, sugar cane and indigo, prosperous plantation owners in South Carolina, Georgia and Louisiana had that kind of money to burn.

The Boston area had numerous reliable sources of ice: Walden Pond in Concord, Fresh Pond in Cambridge, Smith's Pond and Spy Pond in Arlington, Sandy Pond in Ayer, Horn Pond in Woburn, Lake Quannapowitt in Wakefield, Haggett's Pond in Andover, Suntaug Lake in Lynnfield and Wenham Lake in Wenham. If more was needed, any of the innumerable smaller lakes and ponds or the Kennebec and Penobscot Rivers in Maine could be harvested.

In 1801, eighteen-year-old Frederic Tudor (1783–1864) went on a voyage with his invalid older brother, John Henry, sailing from Boston to the southern states and the Caribbean. The heat and humidity ashore and on board proved to be too much for the two northerners. Frederic noted that it taxed his health, but it completely deteriorated John Henry's constitution. He passed away the next year, which emotionally affected Frederic more than a little.

Frederic's father found him a position with family friends who taught him how to trade pimento, nutmeg, sugar and tea. (A graduate of the Boston Latin School, Frederic made the decision at age 13 not to pursue a Harvard education like his older brother William.) Frederic purchased a leather-bound almanac in 1805 and wrote on the cover "Ice House Diary" with a rough drawing of an ice house that resembled the one on his family's farm in Rockwood. The first entry in this journal read: "Plan etc for transporting ice to Tropical Climates. Boston August 1805 William and myself have this day determined to get together what property we have and embark in the undertaking of carrying ice to the West Indies the ensuing winter." Within a few months, he got his cousin James Savage involved, too.

Tudor dipped into his savings and paid for his first brig *Favorite*. (No one in

Boston could be convinced to invest in his scheme let alone carry his cargo). While he waited for winter to set in, someone sent him a brochure about the new refrigerator Thomas Moore invented. His brother William and cousin James went down to Martinique to garner interest. Word got back to Emperor Napoléon Bonaparte, who granted them a monopoly to ship ice to his Caribbean colony.

The *Favorite* left Boston Harbour in February 1806 loaded with 130 tons of ice. About a month later, when it landed in St Pierre, a flaw in the plan became instantly evident: There was no ice house for storing the cargo. Tudor's ice was sold right off the boat: about $50 worth per day. He was offered $4,000 for the entire load, but turned it down, hoping to garner attention with a leaflet campaign. That failed and the ice melted. Tudor was forced to take home a cargo of sugar just to pay the crew. His hope to make $10,000 profit also melted away.

The next year, he sent 180 tons of ice to Havana, Cuba on board the brig *Trident*. He found a ready market. Cuban café owners revelled in the opportunity to serve chilled drinks and ice cream. Tudor sent two more shipments in the

succeeding months, selling $6,000 in product. Unfortunately, he lost his profits again when a cargo of molasses headed to Boston failed to arrive. He also had to cancel a shipment to Martinique, where he had built an ice house that eventually was abandoned.

Why? Because shipments between the United States and the Caribbean became difficult after that: The American government imposed the Embargo Act of 1807 to force Britain to rescind its restrictions on American trade. While the act was in effect, all American cargo for coastal trade had to be bonded at double the value. It also meant Tudor's ship could meet with delays as it made its way down the coast. This was something he could not afford to gamble on. (Luckily this act was repealed two years later so American ships could once again enjoy being the neutral shipping entity while the Napoléonic Wars raged between France and Britain.)

Tudor kept trying, making a little money here and there. In 1810, he caught yellow fever, a tropical disease with no cure. Only the symptomatic relief of ice-pack applications helped the patient until he recovered. Tudor sent his cousin Arthur Savage to Havana with the next ice harvest. He netted $6,400 after $1,000 in expenses. An 1811 Havana shipment put Tudor deep in debt: over $38,000 to Boston investors, his tailor and his blacksmith. His ne'er-do-well younger brother Harry had failed to accept the shipment in time. Tudor, arrested four times for overdue bills, spent parts of 1812 and 1813 in debtors' prison.

This was a stroke of good fortune. The War of 1812 caused even more snags in export shipping than the embargo had. He probably would have lost even more money trying to circumvent the political mayhem that affected international trade with the United States.

Out of prison and ready to start again, in 1815, Tudor managed to borrow $2,100 to buy ice and to build a new ice house in Havana, his most lucrative market: a double-shelled structure with six feet of insulation that could hold 150 tons of ice. "Pursued [in Boston] by sheriffs to the very wharf," Tudor set sail for Cuba on 1 November.

The War of 1812 ended with the ratification of the Treaty of Ghent on 17 February 1816. The seas were free again. Tudor's venture finally was a success, despite a number of bizarre setbacks. He had to invent and construct

individual storage systems because no one was investing in Thomas Moore's refrigerator. But his ice house design let him sell product year round. That same year, the Cuban government granted Tudor a monopoly on the frozen water trade. Tudor was "in the black."

He invested in a new venture the following year, shipping citrus fruits from Cuba to New York aboard the schooner *Parago*, encased in 15 tons of ice and three tons of hay. The fruit rotted during the month-long journey, costing him a $3,000 loan with a 40 percent interest rate and a loss of $2,000.

Tudor was once again deep in debt. The setback didn't stop him. He made his profits from the six shipments totalling 1,200 tons of ice that same year.

Solvent again, he opened up domestic markets in the sweltering hot, tropical-disease prone and cotton-rich/indigo-rich cities of Charleston, South Carolina (1817); Savannah, Georgia (1818); and New Orleans (1821). His marketing scheme offered families regular shipments of ice for a subscription price of $10 a month. He improved his on-board and ice house insulation systems, constructed his own ice houses throughout his market territories and helped create a demand for ice-cold drinks at every port.

Tudor was doing well for himself by 1825, shipping over 4,000 tons of ice in one year. He did even better when he teamed up with Nathaniel Jarvis Wyeth, who came up with a practical way to harness horses to a metal blade to cut ice. Wyeth's ice plow and a few other inventions helped Tudor triple his production. They also led other American inventors to find ways to compete with the natural ice trade – creating artificial ice was the next goal for many. However, Tudor had other plans.

In the spring of 1833, Tudor teamed up with merchant Samuel Austin. They sent 200 tons of ice to Calcutta, India on the brig *Tuscany*. The voyage took 180 days to cross 16,000 miles. At first, the locals thought it was an elaborate hoax when the ship entered the Ganges and word spread of its cargo.

The *Calcutta Courier* reported that: "The Yankees are so inventive, and so fond of a joke at the expense of the old country [England], that we had some misgivings about the reality of brother Jonathan's manifest, and suspected him to be coolly indicting a hoax upon the wonder-loving daughters of Britain."

The temperature that day was over 90 degrees Fahrenheit. The newspaper increased the suspense by reporting how much water was pumped out of the hold while government officials argued about customs duty charges. At the *Calcutta Courier's* and its competitor the *India Gazette's* urging, the ice was declared free of duty and was unloaded in the cool of the night. Although half of the cargo melted during the delay, he made a profit and the venture proved to be an unqualified success.

The British government helped get subscriptions to build a stone ice house in Calcutta so colonists lives could be improved by this miraculous product. It tasted better than the saltpetre and water mixture they usually used to cool wine and beer. Tudor's ice cost half of what it did for the locals to transport ice down from the Himalayas. It was also considerably cheaper than the artificial ice that the natives made. For centuries, locals boiled water in clay pots and rested them in mountain ice until they froze. Then they transported the pots downhill and stored them in dugout cellars for future use.

Calcutta alone yielded Tudor and Austin about $220,000 in profits over the subsequent years. In 1834, they repeated the experiment in a shipment to Rio de Janeiro. With the opening of that monopoly, Tudor was crowned the Ice King of Boston. He had a minor setback when a $200,000 investment in coffee importation failed. But his overall success meant he no longer headed for debtors' prison when he miscalculated.

Now what does the story of the Ice King – and his eventual success – have to do with mixed drinks? As author Gavin Weightman noted in his book The Frozen Ice Trade, thanks to Tudor and his subsequent competitors:

European visitors to Boston, New York, and other cities on the eastern seaboard of the United States could not fail to notice that in the summer there was an awful lot of ice around, and that what was still a rarity and a great luxury on the other side of the Atlantic was considered to be an essential comfort in America. In the streets there were ice carts delivering to hotels and homes, the icemen familiar figures as they hoisted perspiring chunks of crystal upstairs and into doorways with their ice tongs. Water was almost always drunk chilled, and there were many drinks which had crushed ice as an essential ingredient, such as sherry cobblers or mint juleps.

What was once the domain of the very rich or people who lived in subarctic and arctic climates became a true commodity in the world of food and drink. In 1842, a challenger to the Ice King's throne, Jacob Hittinger, secured ice-harvesting rights on Fresh Pond in Cambridge, Massachusetts. He had just formed Gage, Hittinger & Company of Boston. But his sights were set on London, not America or the Caribbean.

Hittinger sent ice via the bark *Sharon* accompanied by a couple of American bartenders to demonstrate how to make Cobblers, Juleps, Smashes and Cocktails. They received a chillier than expected reception.

Then, a New Englander living in London in 1845, Henry Colman, set up the Wenham Lake Ice Company "ice store" on the Strand and offered consumers an opportunity to have ice delivered to their homes by uniformed delivery men. Ice finally caught on in Britain, if only as a passing fad. The price was a little high and the low average temperatures further reduced the allure of ice-cold drinks. However, another wave of interest occurred when the Wenham Lake Ice Company left London and was replaced by Norwegian ice companies who sold their ice for considerably less.

Ice was the hottest trend to hit the world: it was embraced for use in drinks, medical treatment, food preservation and innumerable other practicalities and comforts. But the stories of Tudor, Gage and Hittinger are only the tip of proverbial iceberg.

Back in London in 1834, an American named Jacob Perkins (1766–1849) received a Royal Patent for a "mechanical refrigerator." Perkins was an inventive sort, creating a way to plate shoe buckles, cut and head nails, engrave bank notes, measure the depth of water and measure the speed at which a vessel moves in the water. He even invented an ether-based ice machine. This latest design employed vapour compression instead of chemicals or volatile liquids to produce cold, following the mathematical theories of heat engines laid out in 1824 by French physicist and engineer Nicolas Léonard Sadi Carnot. Sadly, Perkins made only one working refrigerator and never managed to produce a commercial model.

The next person to give it a go was an American physician John Gorrie (1802–1855) who, in 1833, moved to Apalachicola, Florida, where he researched tropical diseases while working in the local hospital. Based on his studies and his foresight, Gorrie urged draining swamps and sleeping under mosquito nets to prevent yellow fever and malaria. He persuaded hospitals to cool patient rooms to reduce fever and to increase comfort levels. Initially, he did this by suspending a basin of ice from the ceiling. Since ice had to be imported from up north, Gorrie tried making artificial ice. Obsessed with his idea, in 1845, he gave up his practice to pursue his vision.

On 6 May 1851, Gorrie was granted a United States Patent #8080 for an ice-making machine. He was unable to raise the funds to commercialise the project after his partner died. Then, Gorrie himself died in seclusion four years later. The nineteenth-century world continued to live on hand-cut ice.

Meanwhile, a new demand for ice surfaced in the United States. Lager beer was introduced to the States around 1840 and quickly captured a large portion of the beer market. The trouble was, lager needed temperatures around 32 to 40 degrees Fahrenheit for fermentation and resting. Lager breweries built underground facilities, took advantage of caves and still required ample supplies of ice to keep up with demand that pushed them to produce in warm weather. Then the lager had to be served colder as well, requiring even more ice.

Ice also had a more solemn use, one that members of the temperance movement were quick to exploit as ice became popular in alcoholic beverages. Ice was placed in coffins to keep bodies chilled during wakes and funeral services. As wakes were often held at home and drinks were frequently served at wakes, these early prohibitionists spread a number of false stories of household servants taking ice from coffins to make cocktails. They also circulated tales of unscrupulous tavern owners and ice merchants picking ice off the ground behind churches after funerals. These tall tales appeared in countless newspapers in the mid-nineteenth century, but did little to curtail people's drinking or their passion for ice in their drinks.

A FRESH GARNISH

Earlier we mentioned that Frederic Tudor attempted to ship tropical citrus fruits from Cuba to New York but failed when the fruit rotted during the month-long voyage. Well, he should have waited three years, used more ice and cut his voyage short by 90 miles or so. He would have had better luck bringing citrus fruits from Florida. In 1819, Spain ceded Florida to the United States, in accordance with the Adams-Onis Treaty, in exchange for the American renunciation of any claims on the territory of Texas. This was the start of a sunny, healthy relationship.

European and colonial American tastes for tropical fruit was whetted long before, when explorers and traders brought tropical fruits back to Europe. It started with Christopher Columbus, who returned with pineapples after his second voyage in 1493. The native Tainos in Guadeloupe were already drinking the juice, which they called *yayamaby*, as a digestive aid. They also used it as a skin lightener. European explorers would soon discover that it added a superb flavour to rum. By the turn of the 19th century ships were arriving at ports such as Marseille and London with cargoes of rum combined with pineapple rinds to produce the desired infusion over the course of the voyage. It became so popular Charles Dickens wrote about it in the Pickwick Papers (1836–1838) and recipes to produce it at home appeared in recipe books as early as 1817.

Oranges were just as exotic, brought from Asia by sea traders who managed to get them to market in Europe before the fruit rotted. Nobility fell so in love with tropical fruits they built orangeries, fitted with water-driven air conditioning and heating, to grow trees in large pots from the few cuttings that survived importation.

The Palace of the Louvre was one of the earliest sites in Europe of a glass-encased, post-Renaissance orangery, built in 1617. Another was built in 1702 at Kensington Palace by Sir Christopher Wren for Queen Anne. Tsar Peter the Great of Russia ordered the Bolshaya Kamennya Oranzherey to be built at Peterhof in 1722. There was one designed by Sir William Chambers built in London's Kew Gardens in 1761. Before long, there were orangeries all over France, England, Poland, Russia, Germany, Austria and Hungary.

People were mad for tropical citrus. They graced the table of any good hostess who could afford to use them as a centerpiece. They were the crowning glory of any good punch. They cost a fortune to obtain even from places like Italy and Spain, where citrus fruits were cultivated by Moors during their occupation of the Iberian Peninsula. The Crusaders imported them between 1000 and 1300.

Limes are indigenous to far-off places like Southeast Asia, the Caribbean and Central and South America. You had to be royalty or at least as rich as a royal from the new-found money in trade and manufacturing to afford these goodies. So citrus didn't become a trendy item until the British East India Company and the Dutch West Indies Company, in the 1600s, made them more readily available. Even then, they cost a pretty penny, especially in the United States. That is, until a remarkable turn of events changed that, opening the citrus market to just about everyone.

Oranges, figs, pomegranates, grapes and other trees were imported to Florida by Spanish explorers. The climate was ideal for oranges and the trees quickly spread beyond the settlements.

Seminole tribesmen cultivated the wild orange groves and introduced them into northern Florida's interior from plantings imported by Ponce de Léon in the 1520s. Colonists led by Menendéz de Aviles in the 1560s brought more plantings.

A shipwrecked party of British colonists documented the existence of numerous citrus trees in 1697, when they made shore in eastern Florida. And when the British took possession of Florida in 1697 (and again in 1763) they found all sorts of citrus varietals in and around the settlement of St Augustine.

Although the French, British and Spanish tried as they might in the ensuing years, they couldn't make a go of farming in Florida: They attempted to grow corn. There were oranges, lemons and limes everywhere. But that didn't really register in any of their minds.

It wasn't until John Moultrie of South Carolina became governor of Florida, just before the American Revolution, that anyone successfully cultivated a pleasure garden of olives, dates, oranges, lemons, limes, citrons, figs, white mulberries, pomegranates, peaches, plums and banana pines near St Augustine. Other British plantation owners also experimented with indigenous plants but everything came to a halt in 1783 when Florida was handed back to the Spanish. A few Americans were admitted to the territory, taking over the old British plantations in eastern Florida. But that was about it.

After the United States gained Florida around 1821 (with future President Andrew Jackson as its governor), settlers cultivated the groves. Interest in oranges and lemons grew, because of their efficacy in treating scurvy. That spurred the development of more groves. Roads were built across the lengthy peninsula and up to Georgia. Waterways were identified and improved. Canals were dug. Coastal harbours were established. Railroads were built with British rails and American cars and engines.

Suddenly, citrus fruits were no longer expensive imports; they were domestic items that were easily transported up the coast and the growing number of professional bartenders readily added them to an expanding repertoire of mixed drinks.

ONLY THE BEGINNING

All of the elements were set in place for the development of a voluminous repertoire of mixed drinks and the creation of a new profession – mixology. But this is not the end of our story: It is only the beginning.

We have explained how the art of distillation and alcohol were born in China as means for preserving the properties of botanicals. We showed how alcohol transformed itself into a way of achieving spiritual oneness with the deities in India before becoming a vehicle for the delivery of medication in Arabia.

A source of scientific intrigue as well as high commerce in the hands European alchemists and traders, alcohol morphed into the element capable of reviving "the energies of modern decrepitude." Aided by explorers, colonists and naval seamen, spirits became a political, social and economic tool. Then they transcended all boundaries and became the foundation of the social equalisers known as the mixed drink and the Cocktail.

But it was two epochal events that occurred back to back, which began with the invention of the Newcomen engine, in 1712, that proverbially put the wheels in motion for the cocktail's true evolution. Just as Gutenberg's movable type and printing press contributed to the spread of distillation throughout the world during the Renaissance, the scientific and technological advances made during the First and Second Industrial Revolutions led to improved production methods and better quality imbibables.

That's where we will pick up our story and take you through to the Cocktail Revival of today. Until then…

Cheers!